The best of Mandy Bolen's

TAN LINES

A hilarious look at Key West and the chaos of everyday life everywhere

PHANTOM PRESS
KEY WEST, FLORIDA

10 9 8 7 6 5 4 3 2 1
December 2003
ISBN# 0-9674498-5-5

The best of Mandy Bolen's

TAN LINES

A hilarious look at Key West and the chaos of everyday life everywhere

PHANTOM PRESS
KEY WEST, FLORIDA

EVERYTHING UNDER THE SUN

ACKNOWLEDGEMENTS

I'm pretty sure the only people who read this page are those who think they'll be mentioned.

There truly is not enough room to thank every person in Key West or elsewhere whose path mine has crossed. Every encounter can become a Sunday column that will make some people laugh and relax, even if it's just for a moment.

And while the chance encounters cannot be scripted, there are some people whose support and patience is steadfast and constant. Without them, this book would not exist.

Above all, thanks to my parents, Bob and Mary Ann Bolen who have been reading my work since I was writing reports about Jupiter on orange construction paper. Hopefully, the work has grown a bit more enjoyable for them to read, but they'll both always remain my first and most important editors.

Thanks to David Sloan, my publisher, but more importantly, my friend, who made me believe a book was possible and made sure it didn't become another file – saved and forgotten in my computer.

If a picture is worth a thousand words, then Rob O'Neal leaves me speechless with his images and the work he puts into capturing them. Thanks for making me look good, Rob.

Thanks to Gregg McGrady, my friend, confidante and local business advisor, who has made sure the books are sold, instead of used for décor in my apartment. And for always being willing to have a cocktail and discuss anything other than my Tan Lines.

And to Joe Weatherby, who survived the glare and clicks of a laptop during countless episodes of "Law and Order," but was always sure it would be worth it.

1,000 WORDS FOR CASUAL

There's more than one guy in this town who cannot tie a tie. I know at least three, and they shall remain nameless.

Some may have learned years ago and since forgotten, while others have never stood in front of a mirror squinting down at two ends of silk.

Growing up in New Jersey, I watched my dad deftly create a double Windsor knot each morning. I saw the guys in my Catholic high school stand in front of their lockers every morning, hurriedly looping the thicker end around the thin before running to homeroom. Even in college, typically an era of baseball hats and T-shirts, the fraternity boys would spruce themselves up once a year for some event requiring a tie and jacket.

But ties are not part of our lives here on this bizarre pendant dangling from a chain of islands, and I rarely hear businessmen complaining about the absence.

Even the poshest of restaurants does not require men to wear a sport jacket, and weddings are so often outdoors that flip-flops take the place of Florsheims and the Ray Bans hanging around the groom's neck replace the tie.

The Keys have amended the dress code for special events to suit our weather, atmosphere and attitude.

Most men in town do not have a tie rack filled with Father's Day gifts. There is a marked absence of shoeshine racks at the Key West International Airport, and ironing boards have become obsolete, replaced by a conveniently located kitchen counter for the odd linen shirt that needs to be ironed before a dinner party.

Then again, I have a friend who uses the Key West humidity to his advantage.

"I don't need a steam iron, I just walk outside in the summertime," he says, examining his white Polo button-down that hangs untucked over a pair of khaki shorts and Birkenstocks.

If the Eskimos have 1,000 words for snow, we have 1,000 words for casual.

Any man with a closet or dresser in Key West has crewneck T-shirts they consider their "good" shirts. Those are the ones, usually a solid color, that are acceptable at outdoor barbecues, happy-hour get togethers and even an occasional work day.

The good T-shirts don't have bar logos on them and are not

bleached with oddly shaped spots. If they are tucked into a pair of khaki pants or shorts, they become an acceptable dinner outfit. The addition of a belt is getting downright elegant.

Of course, for some Keys inhabitants, there could be an annual black tie affair somewhere in town. It's planned by the tiny percentage of people who own their tuxedo and feel the need to wear it within the city limits.

And an occasional suit is visible on Whitehead Street as lawyers and defendants hurry to court.

But let us not focus our attention solely on the male wardrobe. Let's talk pantyhose, ladies (and some men,) and the frequency with which we tug them on. The average year-round temperature here is 77 degrees, according to the mayor's letterhead.

We don't need suntan-colored pantyhose, and we don't need to break a sweat before leaving the house while flailing maniacally with the Sheer Elegance.

Of course, there is always a time and place for appropriate cloth-ing, and if your family is anything like mine, then you have at some point been warned by other family members to dress appropriately for some family function in a place like Connecticut, Wisconsin or New Jersey. I think people in other places live with an innate fear that I will show up at Aunt Millie's funeral wearing a sarong and bikini top while smelling of Coppertone.

While attire is often reflective of someone's personality, we in Key West don't base friendships on whether a woman is wearing hose with a reinforced toe, or whether a man's necktie comes right to his belt buckle.

Shoes don't make a party unforgettable, friendship does. Ties don't make a wedding perfect, love does. Clothes don't make an island alluring, people do. We've created our own dress code, and we look damn good.

August 26, 2001

KEYS, BEADS AND BELONGINGS

photo: roboneal.com

I was sifting through the piles on my dresser the other night and began taking inventory of my life. Relax, it wasn't one of those heavy philosophical inventories like, "What do I want to do when I grow up?" or "What does it all mean?"

It was more like, "What did I do with that overdue sewer bill, how I do repeatedly lose my keys in an apartment this size, and whose phone number did I write on that envelope?"

Shoving aside bills, bank statements, CDs, extra buttons for shirts I no longer own, necklaces and a few books, I started thinking about the possessions that are pretty much universal to residents of this town.

There are certain things we all have. We don't need them, we might not even know we have them. But they're there, and they might never go away.

Take, for example, a quick look in your medicine cabinet, beach bag or patio by the pool. How many varieties of sun products are there? Are you the frugal, sensible type with a full supply of the No-AD sunscreen with an SPF of 15, or is there a dark brown spray bottle advertising a "Tan Accelerator?" Is there a variety of protection levels for out-of-town guests, or just your basic SPF 4 applied so you can feel as if you're doing your skin a favor?

Is there a bottle of green stuff somewhere next to all the sunscreen? We all know that no matter how many times we apply the waterproof lotion, we'll get burned and will need aloe. I keep mine in the fridge for that added cooling sensation on singed shoulders. Sadly, it's often the only thing in my fridge.

But there are usually items hanging on the refrigerator. Many of us never outgrew the thrill of having Mom display our fingerpaintings for all to see. How many newspaper clippings hang on your fridge?

How many people do you know who have been Citizen of the Day, Bartender of the Week or a featured villain in the Crime Report? You've clipped them, displayed them and then either thrown them away, sent them to friends elsewhere in the country, or carefully stowed them in a scrapbook. But they usually start on the fridge.

That brings us to the assortment of other unnecessary, yet universal, items in the kitchen. Admittedly, it's a room in which I spend very little time, but I think most us will admit that somewhere in there exists a tattered red and white China Garden menu.

Say what you will about the differences, real or perceived, between China Garden East and West, Old Town and New, but always order by number and save your egg roll for last.

Moving through the rest of the abode, (told you I don't spend much time in the kitchen) I came to the closet. Shoes spill out no matter how hard I try to keep them organized, but the universal object hangs from a peg toward the back. An old mask and snorkel.

They're not the ones I would use to dive, but are probably the first ones I've owned. I think the snorkel is actually one of the souvenir models from Pennekamp State Park in Key Largo. But don't we all have some version of a snorkel? Whether it's an expensive model used for serious diving, a child's toy for the pool or a supermarket special, the snorkel exists in our lives. We may not remember the last time it was used, and it might only be there for visitors, but there it is in the closet with remnants of salt still visible.

Also in the closet is the shopping bag that only comes out in October. It's filled with a four-year accumulation of beads that become more precious than gold in the final weeks of this month. We all have them, we all clamor for them and we all save the worthless trinkets from year to year. We use them to decorate Christmas trees. We hang them from doorknobs. Or we throw them, in a tangled heap, in a shopping bag in the closet.

But the time is drawing near. Fantasy Fest schedules are spread throughout town. There's talk of floats, masks and costumes. It's time to untangle the baubles – right after I find my keys.

October 7, 2001

Think about it:
According to the 2000 census, there were 79,589 residents of the Florida Keys.

SONGS, SIRENS, SUMMER

Nothing ruins Bruce Springsteen's "Born to Run" more completely, more abruptly than the blue disco lights of a state trooper in your rearview mirror.

I was in the midst of a perfect rendition, complete with a scrunched-up face and an air microphone in one hand while the other kept perfect on the steering wheel. It was the perfect combination of music, a Mustang and summertime all around me. I was wearing faded blue jeans and a white T-shirt and kept one bare foot on the gas pedal.

But the lights behind me were like a needle scratching across the entire album leaving behind a crackling silence barely pulsing with each revolution of the record.

Only I was listening to the Boss on a CD in my rented Mustang the other night on U.S. 1 – and the pulsing was heartbeat. It hammered at my ribcage while I pulled smoothly onto the shoulder cursing myself for accepting the free and zippy upgrade for the drive home from the Fort Lauderdale airport.

Now I'm a sane, fairly law-abiding citizen with a valid driver's license and proof that I had permission to drive the car I was operating. There are no warrants out for my arrest and I wasn't transporting weapons, bodies or kilos of anything in the trunk.

But there I was taking a mental inventory of everything in the car and calculating how long it had been since my last drink – 36 hours. In hindsight, a speeding ticket really was a worst-case scenario, and how bad is that, really?

Rationally, I knew I'd have to really screw up and intentionally spit on the trooper, knock the flashlight out of his hand and open the car door into his groin to break enough laws to warrant a trip to jail.

So why do those flashing lights make us second-guess ourselves and wonder absurdly for a split second if someone has planted contraband in our go-fast rental car?

I couldn't figure it out, so with a sweaty palm I quickly snapped off the tunes, fumbled for my license, turned off the engine and placed both hands on the steering wheel where the officer could see them.

No, I did not summon up tears, bat my eyelashes or make up

some medical condition that forces me to exceed the speed limit. I simply apologized for the oversight and acknowledged that I might have been going a little faster than 55 mph.

Of course, the courteous state trooper knew exactly how much faster than 55 mph I was going, and enlightened me before taking my license and rental agreement back to his car, which was still ablaze with blue lights. Every passing car got a full view of my shame and resignation to an $80 or $100 ticket.

I leaned my head against the back of my seat, kept my hands on the steering wheel and glanced at the turquoise glow from the stereo where Bruce was still belting out tunes at a volume too low to hear.

I thought about how this ticket was going to inevitably affect my insurance premium and how long it would take the trooper to fill in all the lines of the carbon-paper ticket before asking me to sign it and sending me on my way. It does sometimes feels like they purposely take their time writing out the information just to teach us a lesson and negate any progress we made have already made on the road.

But then something wonderful happened. Within minutes the trooper came back to my open window, handed me a "courtesy warning" and told me to drive safely. I vowed solemnly to obey the posted speed limits and told him I would certainly be more careful.

He tipped his hat and allowed me to pull back onto the highway ahead of him. As I turned my attention back to my homeward journey, it was divided between the stereo volume and the rearview mirror, and the gas pedal felt a little more resistant to the pressure from my right foot.

But Bruce was singing a slow song, summertime still surrounded me and I didn't owe the state of Florida any money. Life was good.

August 31, 2003

I'VE GOT MAIL

I was pre-approved for a $10,000 credit line. I may already have won $10 million and was eligible to win a new car simply by ordering a magazine or changing my long distance provider – all in one afternoon.

The excitement at my mailbox was almost too much to bear. But it was quickly tempered by the less glossy more serious-looking envelopes that contained a cell phone bill, an electric bill and a car insurance bill.

In all fairness to my car insurance company, they did send a sheet of adhesive return address labels just to thank me for being a valued customer during this holiday season. (I'd feel more valued if they decided that I was such a swell customer, I could skip this quarter's payment "just to thank me for being a valued customer this holiday season.") But there was no such correspondence in my mailbox, so the check's in the mail, State Farm.

Despite the bills, I must say I enjoy checking my mailbox each day. It's one of the few daily rituals that still holds some surprise, and there's so many different types of it.

We've already covered the necessary evil of bills, and, I've discovered that the "out of sight, out of mind" trick actually works when the bills are piling up and funds in the checking account are not. Just leave the bills in the mailbox until you're to ready to pay them. It works better than having to look at them on the coffee table every time you set a drink down.

But I like having catalogs to set on the coffee table. I rarely order anything, but I do enjoy thumbing through them. Some people opt to keep the catalogs in that magazine rack they keep in their bathroom, but the coffee table works for me. The best part about catalogs is getting new ones when you move. The post office generally won't forward catalogs, so when I moved into my place I started getting the previous tenants' catalogs and shortly discovered that they made more money than I.

Do you ever look at the missing kids flyers? It's the least I can do. So far, I've never recognized anyone, but you never know.

Bank statements are boring, and I usually throw them away unopened – unless there's some demand that I open it immediately. That usually indicates some additional fee the bank took out of my account for something they think is a justified reason to screw me out of my own money.

Greeting cards addressed in someone's own handwriting rather than a computer-generated label are always fun. I love it when people care enough to send the very best. My mom's really good at sending thoughtful cards at random times, so are some of my best out-of-town friends. Cards are nice, and are one of my favorite mailbox surprises.

Of course, a check or some cash inside makes for an even better surprise, but I don't often get my hopes up for that anymore.

Birthday and Christmas cards from my high school and college generally include pleas for money, and are no fun, but I do like getting the alumni newsletters from both schools. I always flip to the year of my graduating class to see who's gotten married, who's working where and who surprised everyone by finishing law school.

Ever notice that the ones still working at the local movie theater and going to the same bar we needed fake IDs for never respond to those newsletter surveys?

Kids are being born left and right in my extended family these days, so I'm getting a photo birth announcement at least once a month. I can't keep all my new first cousins, once removed, straight anymore. At least I'm not expected to remember their birthdays with greeting cards and enclose a check.

Packages are the best form of mail in the world, although they can be disappointing when you discover the little brown box only contains the checks the bank has already charged you for.

But apparently, I'll get more packages if I accept the credit card with the $10,000 credit line, use it to buy a bunch of stuff from the expensive catalogs and then pay the bill with my new checks – until the bank statement comes telling me I have overdrawn my account and I owe the bank more of my money. But that's okay. I may have already won $10 million.

January 5, 2002

HMMMM...

How many people have gotten splinters in their mouth from Popsicle sticks?

In such a safety-conscious society (my hair dryer tells me not to use it in the bathtub) we continue the barbaric practice of putting frozen fruit flavors on flattened sticks that really aren't all that smooth.

Don't get me wrong, I love Popsicles, and wouldn't want to see them changed. Apparently, I'll just have to be a bit more careful.

But it surprises me that the same government that puts warning labels on rubber bands doesn't see anything wrong with Popsicle sticks. There's a warning on those chicken Kiev things when toothpicks are used to keep the rolled-up ingredients together.

Also, why can't Laundromats come up with some universal pricing and timing system?

Sometimes it takes eight quarters (40 minutes) to dry a load of clothes, but at other times and places, it only takes six quarters. Of course, if it's a load of towels and jeans, it's going to cost you $2.50.

A little uniformity would be nice in the chaotic world of laundry, that's all. For those of us without the privilege of a washer and dryer in our homes, someone could make the nightmarish task a little more pleasant. It's bad enough that you often lug your clothes to the Laundromat with a pocketful of quarters only to find that all but one dryer is out of order and someone spilled Tide all over the washer lid.

And then, without fail, you end up dropping a sock somewhere en route from dryer to folding table, so by the time you get home, you forever are left with an odd number of socks.

And while I'm asking questions no one can answer, how much weight do we lose each time we urinate?

I'm sure it must vary from time to time, but I'm serious. There's a certain volume of liquid that was once in our bodies and is no longer there. That volume of liquid weighs something, so I figure going to the bathroom is a sort of weight-loss program. Imagine how much weight I must lose on the nights I consume several 12-ounce bottles of beer and use the bathroom every five minutes?

Do I look thinner yet?

Is it possible to drink enough non-alcoholic beer to reach the point of impairment? I'm not saying this is something we should try, have you ever tasted that stuff? But I figure, there is some amount of alcohol, by volume, in that "near beer."

So, how many would it take to get drunk? I have plenty of friends who have said it's physically impossible, but it seems to me it could happen. Besides, my friends are pretty much unfamiliar with anything non-alcoholic. Hell, I had friends in high school who drank Robitussin "just to see what would happen."

They're all either in jail or rehab now, except for one, who's a pharmacist.

How come fake butter is so much easier to spread than real butter?

I must say I enjoy the taste of real butter more than that of the processed, whipped vegetable oil. But the fake stuff spreads so nicely onto an English muffin that I find myself sacrificing taste for spreadability.

I realize the ingredients are different and all, but it seems a bit unfair. I keep them in the same refrigerator and spread them onto muffins and toast that is the approximate same temperature when it comes out of the toaster oven.

And I've tried keeping a stick of butter in a dish on my kitchen counter so it stays soft. This is Key West and the stick was a puddle by midday.

Do bald people use shampoo?

Do they rub it all over the top of their head, or does a bar of soap work just as well?

What's the fastest way to fill up an ice cube tray?

Is it quicker to move the tray back and forth under the running water filling each little rectangle individually, or should you hold the tray in one place and tilt it under the faucet so the first two compartments get filled and then overflow into the rest of them?

Oh, and what's the easiest way to get a splinter out of your lower lip?

June 8, 2003

15

photo: roboneal.com

I had to step over an unconscious man who had spilled his beer and wet his pants in order to get to my front door a few months ago.

No, it was not a friend of mine who had started happy hour before noon. (My friends know where the key is hidden, usually make it up the steps before collapsing and tend not to urinate on themselves.)

He was face down on the sidewalk, a can of Natural Ice spilled just inches from the curled fingers of his right hand.

With my arms filled with files and a Fausto's grocery bag dangling from a forearm, I instinctively held my breath as I approached. I knew the assaulting fume would be the unmistakable combination of filth, body odor, urine, booze and mildew that comes from damp clothes being worn week after week in the Key West humidity.

I gave the guy a wide berth and climbed the steps, happy to be home after a long day at work.

If this column were meant to be a sympathetic commentary about the plight of the homeless, then here's where I would write about how I then stopped in a moment of enlightenment on the seventh step, and looked back down. I'd say how I then brought down a plate of food for the filthy man in his late 30s.

But this isn't one of those columns. I've written enough of them. And I didn't offer any food to the guy on the sidewalk because the last time I tried that, the intended recipient gave me the finger and asked for a cigarette.

Instead, I called the cops. A string of profanity about the courteous officer, his mother and career choice continued as the sidewalk sleeper stumbled halfway down the sidewalk and scratched himself.

On that day my sympathy and desire to help had given way to anger and resentment, partly because so many don't seem to want help. I applaud the homeless who utilize the job placement services offered at various centers around town. I appreciate the work being done at St. Mary's Soup Kitchen, which provides clean clothes for job interviews and hot meals, rather than beer money. Congratulations to the people who actively seek to get off the street.

But I don't see too many who want to work. It's easier to hold a sign asking for beer money, or funds to continue marijuana research. Cute. But how about getting a job, scumbags?

That's right a job, also known as work, employment or an occupation for which one receives a regular paycheck of some amount. The money can be used to acquire soap. Amazingly enough, these people with jobs and paychecks often have a little money left over to buy Natural Ice rather than asking others for money.

Yes, I had run out of sympathy and was, instead, disgusted. I was disgusted that this has become an accepted part of life in this town. Disgusted that taxpaying residents have to hold their breath in front of their own home. Disgusted that the police officer who came by had already performed the same duty five times that evening.

Ever walked through the library on a hot August afternoon? They set up camp in the newspaper section, relish the air-conditioning and subsequently repulse anyone trying to browse the bookshelves. Are our kids now going to equate libraries with the smell of bums sleeping behind newspapers? That's great.

Here's where I should be prepared to offer a solution. I regret that I cannot. I don't know the answers, but I do respect the people trying to find them.

Parents can't take their kids to the beach without seeing the homeless sprawled on the picnic tables. Tourists can't wander along Duval Street without being asked for change, and while it's often entertaining to come up with snide responses to their requests, the situation is out of control.

"A good friend mastered the response to, "Can you spare some change?"

He replies, "Change comes from within."

I don't particularly care where it comes from, but change needs to come from somewhere in this town, and it should not be used for Natural Ice.

November 24, 2002

INHALING DUVAL

photo: roboneal.com

A friend of mine was denied his chance at "Citizen of the Day" fame a few years back. He gave what was considered an inappropriate response to the daily question, "What do you like best about living in the Keys?"

His reply of "the smell of Duval Street in the morning," while not a Tourism Development Council-approved statement, would have elicited more than one wry chuckle on page 3 the next morning. And it would have been more inspired than the monotonous "people, weather and laid-back atmosphere" response.

But as said friend was relating his tail of rejection, I began actually to ponder the various aromatic nuances of our fair island's legendary road.

Of course, there are discernible differences between afternoon and nighttime smells on Duval Street. Picture a cloudless day in March somewhere around the 500 block near Fast Buck Freddy's.

As throngs of college kids saunter past in a sunburned frenzy to catch an afternoon snorkel boat, Wayne's lemonade stand on Fleming Street sends ripples of sweet citrus into the intersection.

The crowds on Duval, co-eds and cruise ship shoppers, radiate the almost-perfect scent of sunscreen and coconut oil – until something else invades your nostrils.

Some of the island's young, hygienically challenged dog owners breeze by with oversized pants, homemade tank tops and dreadlocks.

The litany of inhaled fragrances changes after sunset, as blackening spices meet various filets, as Angelina's cranks out hundreds of pizzas for the now sun-soaked snorkelers and as Mangoes' outside chefs throw magnificent amounts of garlic into sauté pans by the pizza oven.

But as dinner dissolves into cocktails and the smell of sunscreen is replaced by the cooling scent of aloe, a heady mixture of perfume and cologne collide.

Nowhere is the cologne more apparent than in the intersection of Petronia and Duval – there's a higher concentration of men here. And I'm willing to bet most of them have an impressive collection of designer bottles arrayed neatly on a stylishly metallic bathroom counter.

The scent of the night can mix pleasantly with night-blooming jasmine and a passing woman's Alfred Sung perfume, but as last call approaches, the sweet scents seem to fade like a co-ed's make up, replaced by the nasal-assaulting factors that continue until the early-morning hours.

The rare wanderers who've traversed lower Duval anytime between 5 and 9 a.m. know the unmistakable and sadly unforgettable smell that seeps from between the buildings and oozes from the ever-present liquid pooled in the crumbling part of Charles Street.

Keep in mind, your opinion of a morning on Duval does not count if you're there without first having gone to bed. (I have never done this, Mom.) By the time you've spent all night there, that blessed phenomenon known as olfactory overload kicks in – it's the same quality that allows Key deer to live happily in that one area of Big Pine.

By 6 a.m. the smell of beer, no longer just flat, now heats up in puddles and mixes with the fermenting cream from an unfinished Mudslide. There's the occasional whiff of trash and bodily fluids – and the hippies still haven't showered.

But by 9 a.m., crews have emptied the trashcans and swept the sidewalks. A light breeze has jostled the air and a living saint is somewhere making coffee. The sun exacerbates hangovers, but coaxes the snorkelers from hotel beds. The scent of Coppertone again fills the air as Wayne squeezes his first lemon, and somewhere a Citizen photographer is looking for a Citizen of the Day.

January 27, 2002

Think about it:
A bloodhound's sense of smell is
1,000 times better than that of a human.

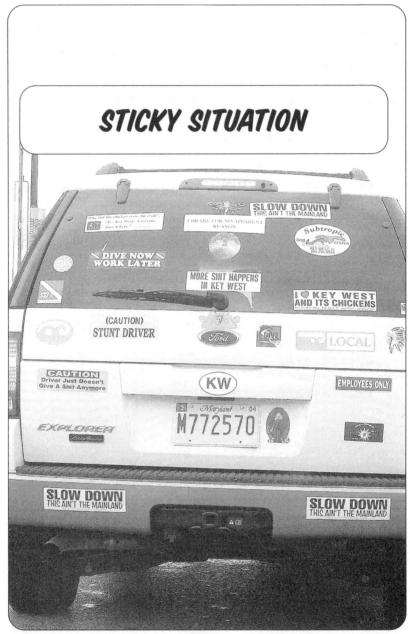

photo: roboneal.com

Do you do it?

I don't, but I'm glad other people do.

We're talking about bumper stickers here, for any of my otherwise-minded readers who were beginning to think sick thoughts. Some people opt to affix sarcastic, sappy and self-deprecating stickers on the back of their vehicles, and I want to thank them.

The 40 seconds spent at a red light in the middle of a hectic afternoon are often infused with humor and a new perspective because the guy in front of you stuck a, "Would-you-drive-better-if-I-shoved-your-phone-up-your-ass?" bumper sticker on the back of his truck.

I want to thank that man for changing my day last week. And no, I don't think the phone's new position would improve my already-questionable driving skills.

But the sticker, accompanied by one that read, "You should be the poster child for condoms," did remind me to turn the radio up loud enough to drown out the cell phone ringing in my purse.

Every once in a while I find myself stopped behind someone who does it – a lot. Their station wagon (it's always a station wagon) is wallpapered with stickers and decals of all colors and attitudes. They give you, in the time it takes to place a drive-thru order, an adhesive slice of the driver's life. But even single bumper stickers placed carefully on the back of cars and trucks offer some insight about the driver.

Take, for example, a few of the stickers seen commonly around town, and consider their implications.

"Slow down, this ain't the mainland" translates to "I'm probably not a Conch, but have lived here long enough to form an opinion while realizing that despite my complaints, I couldn't live anywhere else."

"Porn Star" bumper stickers could lose something in the translation, but usually belong to either a gay or straight male somewhere in his mid to late 20s. He owns at least one article of clothing from Abercrombie and Fitch and has been "clubbing" at some point.

"I'm not gay but my boyfriend is," is easily interpreted to mean, yes, the driver is most likely a homosexual man.

"PLAYSOCCER," is often seen on the back of a minivan or SUV. The acronym for American Youth Soccer Organization helps with the analysis. The driver has kids who play soccer, duh. Do they give these stickers out at soccer registration each year?

"Jesus is my co-pilot," is used by a person who probably drives worse than me, but feels safer doing it.

"My president is Charlton Heston" sticker-bearers almost certainly own firearms, and could very well have it stowed under the seat. Try not to rear-end them.

An "I'd rather be fishing," driver is probably male who enjoys fishing. Again, duh.

But this brings us to the question of bumper sticker origins. Do the drivers buy them? Are they given as gifts or picked up for free somewhere?

Did the fishing sticker come from a cherished grandson, or was it on a give-away table at a rod and reel expo? Do people buy bumper stickers for themselves, or do their friends seek out the most fitting mottos and hand them over?

Regardless of how they get there, I'm glad they exist. Everyone reads bumper stickers. Be they politically argumentative, lewd, earthy and encouraging or downright insulting, they are placed there purely for the benefit of others' road reading. The one I saw the other day was truly meant to protect the driver's fellow motorists.

"I roll back on hills," appeared on the rear windshield of a VW Bug. I smiled as I kept my distance at the inclined Wendy's drive-thru.

I may never do it, but I hope some people never stop.

December 2, 2001

Think about it:
When Ernest Hemingway's good friend, Gertrude Stein, first read a draft of "The Sun Also Rises," she told the Key west author to "start over again, and concentrate." And he did.

MONEY MATTERS

There were two of us in line behind her, and she was taking too long. We all needed cash. It was apparent from the way we stood several feet back from the cash machine giving her the privacy needed to type in four secret digits.

We were prepared to wait the three and a half minutes it takes to enter a PIN, choose either checking or savings, enter an amount and then retrieve the bills. But we were not patient enough to stand in the unrelenting sun while she recounted the stack of 20s, tucked the bills neatly into her wallet and rooted through her purse to find a pen with which to write the withdrawal into her checkbook. She did all this while standing directly in front of the machine, where the sun was not in her eyes and that thin little stream of cool air often escapes from the bank building behind the machine.

We stood, two strangers on a sidewalk, united in disgust at this woman in the too-tight pants with a deluxe leather checkbook cover.

Let's face it, we all need cash, and the advent of the Timeless Teller, Green Machine, MAC, Cash Cow and ATM has made our lives easier. But there are some universal matters of etiquette and operation that must be addressed before someone like the woman in the bad pants gets hurt.

First, you do not balance your checkbook, write down your withdrawal or reorganize your wallet while standing in front of a money machine that has a line forming. These financial responsibilities are best addressed when seated back in the comfort of an air-conditioned car, or hastily scribbled while walking away from the machine.

I'm particularly sensitive to these withdrawal writers and their delays mainly because I don't write down my withdrawals – ever. If money comes out of the machine after I've entered my information, I'm all set, at least for as long as that $40 lasts.

Of course, there are those trying times when the machine begins printing out a receipt before you hear the reassuring shuffle of money inside, which means the receipt will say something about the amount entered exceeding the funds available. I swear there are times I can actually hear the machine chuckling as if to say, "You've got to be kidding. You know as well as I do there is no money in this account, so just go on home and watch a rerun of "Friends."

Aside from the time limit I think should be imposed at all ATMs, (and by the way, it is not an ATM machine. The 'm' already stands for 'machine,' dummy) there is the question of space. How far back is an acceptable distance to wait for the person in front of you? I think we tend to exaggerate the space needed to protect someone's privacy. The sun glare that normally falls on most ATM screens in this town, coupled with the small buttons and the user's position directly in front of said buttons makes it difficult to interpret the person's PIN. (Again, the 'n' already stands for number.)

And how ridiculous do we make ourselves look trying so hard to seem nonchalant while waiting to use the machine? We stand there, usually with our card in hand, kicking at the sidewalk, crossing and uncrossing our arms and looking from the sky to our card, which we tend to flick with our thumb and middle finger. I can't explain our actions, I just write about them.

Another thing, how many people trust the machine enough to make a deposit in that envelope and slot? Not me.

And did you ever hit the button for Spanish when you don't speak Spanish? It's harder than you'd think to navigate the screens.

And the fees charged by the machine that are "in addition to any other fees charged by my financial institution?" Please.

I think the fees should only be charged to people who take too long – like the woman in the ugly pants, for example.

May 5, 2002

Think about it:
The average American uses an ATM about five times per month.

MI CASA ES SU CASA

There are 19 drinking vessels in my apartment. None of them were clean.

They weren't all in the sink awaiting the soap and sponge, but were scattered from the dresser in my bedroom to the rattan table on the porch, and I noticed one of the plastic ones in my car the other day.

There are seven bath towels – plenty for one person who does laundry every 10 days. (Hey, they dry quickly outside on the porch, and don't try to tell me you've never reused a towel.) But with three people using them, the stack of fresh linens quickly diminished. The towels ended up tossed over chairs, hanging behind doors and waving like terry cloth flags from the railing facing Simonton Street – probably some sort of historic-district violation.

Ten different shoes were strewn throughout the house, not including the other 30 or so still in the closet. Most were flip-flops, some were sneakers, none was within seven feet of its mate.

The coffee table was moved nightly to make room for the metallic contraption known as the pull-out couch. Once deployed, the device takes up 70 percent of the living room, which also becomes the closet, bedroom and breakfast nook for those treasured visitors who are our houseguests.

I know I'm not alone in recounting a tale of recent visitors. Last weekend was Easter, and we all have friends whose kids were on vacation. We all have friends who are teachers on spring break. We all have friends who aren't teachers, but still cling to the dream that they can come down here and mingle with the college students without looking creepy and old. (News flash, guys: You do look creepy drinking scotch while watching the wet T-shirt contests, and you are getting old.)

In my case, the five days of chaos in my apartment was not nearly enough time spent with friends I've known since my first year of college in North Carolina, where Anna and I were roommates and where we both met Andy, the quiet musician who would become her other half.

The happy couple drove down from Long Island and arrived, honking, late Thursday night. The car was unloaded into the living room that quickly began to resemble our college residence, which, rumor has it, has since been condemned.

Anna's and Andy's New York pallor quickly gave way to mild

sunburn that had settled into a golden bronze by Monday afternoon. The sky was cloudless except for a short morning shower that didn't even delay our breakfast, and there was always a breeze on the beach.

The water lapped gently at the sand at Fort Zach, where we all sat, silently reading in the familiar comfort that requires no conversation.

The sun fell from the sky each night while we watched, laughingly sipping frozen drinks adorned with impossibly large chunks of tropical fruit. The sweet concoctions eventually gave way to beers as we settled in for those Key West nights that don't end until morning – just hours before the snorkel boat is supposed to leave the dock.

Saturday night, unfortunately, hindered Andy's enjoyment of the blue water that undulated before us on the catamaran. But he managed to get into the water for a bit and enjoy the visibility that was unexpectedly great despite high winds and waves.

Nothing but land will cure seasickness, and Andy was thrilled when back on solid ground, where he promptly took a nap before starting his final evening in Key West. It proved to be significantly more tame than the previous one, although in the morning, the living room still was littered with remnants of our activities.

Amid the backpacks, CDs, beer bottles, towels and sunscreen emerged the friendship that will last forever – and a pile of laundry that could take just as long to wash.

April 7, 2002

Think about it:
Key West singer, Lenore Troia, is known locally for her song, "Everyone has a Houseguest in Key West."

A MOVING EXPERIENCE

Someone is always moving in this town.

There must be some statistic aimed to boggle the mind stating that in Key West, a lease is signed every eight seconds.

I know three people who moved in the past two weeks. Actually, it was six people vacating three apartments. But either way, moving can be categorized in two ways – moving, and helping others move.

Let's not kid ourselves, they both suck. But they are unique experiences completely different from each other – aside from the heavy lifting in the heat, which is pretty much universal. And each comes with its own set of advantages and disadvantages.

Moving comes with tiny thrills of discovery, like when you realize the light switch in the bedroom, for some reason, controls the ceiling fan in the living room. Or when you learn there are already nails and hooks in the walls on which to hang pictures and then find an extra electrical outlet in the closet.

Nope, you'll never use that outlet and will forget it's there as soon as the shoes are unpacked, but you found it and if you ever feel the need to blow dry you hair while choosing an outfit, you'll know it's possible.

Also, the first night in a new place is great. Your sheets on your bed with your pillows fill the room that really won't feel like it belongs to you until you wake up and throw that first pile of dirty clothes into some corner that will then forever be designated as the laundry corner.

Perhaps even more rewarding is the first night of order in the new place. Going to sleep and knowing there are no more boxes to be unpacked in the living room is an accomplishment. The dishes are arranged neatly and conveniently in the kitchen, books line the shelves and art is in place on the walls. The place is yours and the work is over – until the landlord decides to sell the property to people who buy the whole thing, use it for two weeks each year and never rent it out.

But until that first night of order, the act of moving is one not generally enjoyed, and changing homes is fraught with frustration.

Forget about the hours spent circling classified ads and leaving messages on answering machines practically begging people to let you see the space they have to offer.

Moving Day brings with it the task of begging friends to help. All of a sudden, friends who have trucks become much more attractive than they were a week ago. Once you enlist the aid of three able if not willing chums, it's your responsibility, as the person moving, to pay for the booze and pizza that inevitably follow a day of heavy lifting.

Also, you're left to unpack the hundreds of boxes, crates and laundry hampers your fine friends have piled into your new place. As soon as the pizza disappears, and they have enough of a buzz, those friends leave you in your new place and go in search of something fun to do.

And their idea of fun does not include navigating the miserable labyrinth of public utilities and government employees while trying to get your phone number and electricity transferred to your new address without leaving yet another $150 deposit, which you still never got back from your very first apartment.

No, the friends who helped have their own list of complaints that always begins with some sort of moaning about how heavy a pull-out couch can possibly be. The unpaid movers also contend, usually at high volumes, with narrow and tricky staircases and landings, paying minimal attention to any damage wrought on walls that are not theirs.

On the other hand, helping a friend move is indeed rewarded with food and frosty adult beverages, although often the refrigerator is not yet up and running, so you have to drink fast and make a hasty escape, silently thrilled that you don't have to deal with the snarl of electrical wires that will somehow, someday, make television, movies, phone messages and e-mail possible.

And let us not forget that helping someone move pretty much obligates them to do the same when you move – in about eight seconds, statistically speaking.

September 1, 2002

FANTASIES (LOST)

Checked your pockets yet? Have you managed to pry your tongue from the roof of your mouth and turn your head far enough to determine where your purse, keys and shoes ended up? (Oh, never mind, you're still wearing your shoes. That's OK, it happens.) Or are you still lying face down, sideways across your bed with your shoes on and feathers from a lost boa stuck to your face? That's OK, too, but at some point we all have to graduate to the upright position, take inventory and determine what was lost last night in the frenzied chaos that was Fantasy Fest.

Last year, a friend of mine lost his scooter for three days and found it on the Wednesday after the parade parked delicately on someone's front porch – six steps above the ground.

I lost my leather whip one year. Hey, it was the year of the circus theme and I was a lion tamer. Of course, by about 1 a.m. no one seemed to care what I was, only that I was dangerously close to flicking their eyeballs out with a cracking strip of leather. (I didn't actually lose the whip, a friend confiscated it to protect those around me.)

Few of us manage an entire Fantasy Fest night on Duval Street without losing something, and right about now, on Sunday, is when we all figure out what we're missing.

By now some of us are panicked while looking through pockets and purses for the essentials – ATM card, driver's license and any left over cash. If they're all there, we're doing OK – unless we realize we've lost one or more undergarments, and along with them, the memory of where we last saw them.

Parts of our costume that weren't attached to us are probably gone by now – boas, wigs, masks, that stuff. Even some costumes that were attached, like body paint, are also missing. Some of the paint was left on the curb where that woman fell down in front of The Bull. And some of it was, and this is just a guess, left on the sheets of the guy who helped her up and bought her her next drink.

Somebody lost a girlfriend last night.

Either they became inadvertently separated, or she refused to believe that it was really his first time in a gay bar – singing along with

Cher and borrowing another man's body glitter.

The people asleep on the couches in hotel lobbies and curled up in pool chairs are the ones who lost their room keys – or their girlfriend, who may have been carrying said room key.

And some of the ones in jail are the ones who lost that mental filter that allows us to distinguish between things we should and should not say to police officers.

The cop may have ignored the first comment about his mother and even the second. He may also have overlooked the Fat Tuesday cup filled with purple grain alcohol. But with the complete loss of that filter between thought and word came the barrage of slurred threats, denials and accusations, all muttered through the blatantly dilated pupils that eventually could not be ignored. And those who lost that filter better hope their significant other didn't lose the ATM card.

Oh, and for those of you still struggling to stand upright while wondering why the sun has to be so bright on this tropical island, you might not realize what you lost until bits and pieces of the evening and early morning come flooding back in horror-movie detail. And then you realize – it's your dignity. It went the way of your inhibitions sometime around 3 a.m. and you might never find it again, although you might look for it on your friend's videotape, which ironically, never seems to get lost.

You'll probably never find your dignity, but it's OK, it'll be fun to lose it again next year.

Thanks for another year of memories. Cheers!

October 26, 2003

Think about it:

The hand dryer in the men's bathroom at the Green Parrot Bar in Key West is so strong, it once blew all the Jack Daniel's and Diet Coke out of a patron's cup. (Trust us on this one.)

E-FILE...YEAH, RIGHT

Go ahead, give it a shot. File your tax return online – the company that's charging $19.99 for the use of their online tax software told me the process was quick and easy.

Liars.

I consider myself a reasonably capable human being – I have a job, a college degree and have almost figured out how to change the channel using that complicated silver remote that came with my friend's satellite dish.

I admit, I cheated my way through physics and calculus. But I figured as long as the 1040 form doesn't require me to remember that force = mass x acceleration or determine the derivative of some number, then I should be able to enter the numerical figures from certain boxes on my W-2 (the form that always reminds you of the money you made, but apparently, and unknowingly, spent.)

So I tried.

Me, an English major who owes at least part of my college scholarship to math whiz Andrew Lund (God, I hope he shows up at some reunion), I logged on and threw myself into the online tax service.

They're really nice...in the beginning. They ask easy questions like your name and address, and build your confidence by asking you to match the figures from the W-2 boxes to the boxes on the screen.

Again, easy enough.

But then something went horribly awry.

I won't go into the gory details, but it must have had something to do with me agreeing to have the computer program "import" some of the same information they had saved from last year's attempt, which included a bunch of different forms. In addition to the W-2, I had a 1099-R, a 1099-MISC and a few others from jobs I'm not even sure I had.

Apparently, the computer assumed I had received the same forms this year.

Chaos ensued.

I had eight errors in my tax return file once I had completed all the questions and checked all the boxes. Of course, the error page seems to shout at you while coming up with all sorts of warnings about false filings and incorrect reported income.

By 8 p.m. I was convinced the knock on my door was from someone in a dark suit preparing to confiscate my computer and W-2 and then shoot me in the kneecaps.

The errors all came from the information I had "imported" for my convenience. Thanks for nothing.

The computer was convinced I had a pile of additional forms in front of me and was simply choosing not to enter the information from them into the program this year. Of course, once I figured out the root of the problem, I tried everything to "un-import" the information, or simply explain to the experts that there were no other forms and no information was missing.

I was alone and bereft of any guidance. I used the back and forth arrows to try to find the imported information. I even clicked the Help button, and selected the topic that most closely resembled my problem – nothing. I then looked desperately for a phone number. Horror!

I realize in this day and age we should be able to do everything from taxes to pizza delivery online without ever having to communicate verbally with another human being.

But would it be so hard to have an 800 number at the top of the screen? Staff it with one person who knows what they're talking about and who will only agree to speak with you once you've exhausted all online Help options.

I'd be fine with that. I'd be willing to admit defeat as long as a human voice told me it's okay that my forms have changed since last year. But there was nothing. Not even someone to congratulate me on attempting to do the whole process online so as not to subject our IRS employees to possible paper-cuts. No one to smile proudly at me for beginning the task three months before the national deadline.

So I did what I thought best. I turned off the computer without saving my work, poured a glass of wine and ordered a pizza – with a telephone. Sadly, the guy who answered wasn't able to reassure me about having different tax forms from last year, but he did give me a free order of cinnamon sticks.

January 19, 2003

FACES I KNOW, PEOPLE I NEED

I don't know his name.

He lives half a block away and I see him everyday – the black man in the blue jeans, always reclining comfortably on a knapsack, legs outstretched, face pensive.

We've nodded in mutual recognition and said good morning, but I've never asked his name. I passed him the other day en route to the post office, right before I saw Wayne selling lemonade by Fast Buck's and just after hanging up from one of the most familiar voices in my life.

On a small island, there are people we see everyday, once a week, a few times a month, or a few times each year. We develop relationships of varying degrees with these people who become part of life in unique ways.

There are vague acquaintances whose names we may or may not know. We encounter them in different places, and usually have a similar conversation each time we see them. Maybe we have a mutual friend whom neither has seen in ages.

"Hi, how's it going?"

"Great, and you?"

"Seen [insert name here] recently, I haven't heard from him in ages. Is he still in town?"

"No clue, haven't seen him since before Christmas last year. Are you still working at [insert job here]?"

"Yep. You still at the paper?"

The familiar exchange usually ends with someone looking at their watch, pretending to suddenly remember something important that requires immediate attention. You walk away promising to get together sometime.

Then there are the people who become involved in your life merely because of their occupation. Bartenders are a prime example. Some know my name, others just my drink order. Many are true friends who would be having a drink with me if they were on the same side of the bar, while others are simply the friendly keepers of cold beers.

Real conversations about work, love, new apartments and old complaints are born between songs and during the blessed silence that envelopes the bar when orders for pina coladas temporarily subside.

Unfortunately, these treasured pleasantries between friends can be interrupted by someone you would rather never see again. Sure, it is a town known for tolerance, but there are some intolerable people and we are not bound by any laws to like them.

The unplanned meetings with such individuals are made significantly more unpleasant if the dreaded person has had more than two drinks.

"These are the times that try men's souls," and test the fake smile that's been perfected over time. A strained semblance of conversation takes place while you look beseechingly toward the bartender who has the power to dramatically increase his tip by interrupting the conversation with a well-timed, "Oh, hey, Mandy, I forgot to tell you."

If this doesn't happen, the fake smile turns into a grimace just before you say, "Hey, it was good seeing you, I have to use the restroom."

You walk to the bathroom, taking care to bring your cash, drink and any other possessions knowing full well you will not be returning to that seat.

But there are times spent with true friends that make everything else seem manageable. Those friends are the ones who know which individuals you have deemed intolerable and will warn you of their presence long before a conversation becomes necessary.

Those friends know when you've had a rough day, and take it upon themselves to order you a drink and listen. They'll lend you $100 until payday, and notice new shoes. They call during a storm to remind you thunder can't hurt. They roll their eyes but tolerate your neurotic idiosyncrasies. They stay up all night when you're sick. Hell, they stay up all night when you're feeling great. They let you cry, and then make you laugh until you almost wet your pants.

They help you move when they can think of 47 ways they'd rather spend a hot Saturday afternoon. They make decisions when your mind is incapable. They know you'd be lost without them, but they make you feel like the most important person in the world. They are friends, they are precious and they might even know the name of the man half a block away.

September 9, 2001

KILLING TIME

photo: roboneal.com

Name four streets in town that begin with the letter "A." We'll all handily rattle off three, but which do we pick for the fourth? And don't forget about Ashby and Alberta.

Now name 20 streets that are women's first names – I promise there are at least that many. I was bored enough to jot them down on the margin of the legal pad on which I started this train of thought, which (warning) will not be the express route to a point.

I also came up with six streets that share the same name as American presidents, and no, North and South Roosevelt boulevards are not counted separately. Are you forgetting Johnson or Washington Street?

This little trivia game, albeit slightly pathetic, is actually an entertaining way to pass the time – as long as you're with friends and have access to booze.

Seriously, I sat in the Chart Room a year or so ago with three friends. We had already discussed all the legends inside the old bar at the Pier House Resort, our thumbs were starting hurt from cracking open peanuts and we had not yet been thrown out.

So we started our local geography lesson. Of course, it eventually evolved into an argument about whether Petronia is a woman's name, which spelling of Frances signifies a female and a reminder that there was no President Duncan.

But we branched out from street names during our games and moved on to recent history. (It was best this way since we had been drinking and local historian Tom Hambright would not have wanted to hear from us at that hour asking him to settle a bet about Old Key West.)

Besides, our group was much better at recent Key West history than, say, prehistoric history. (Try saying Paleolithic or triceratops after several cocktails.)

We stuck to stuff like, what's the name of the creepy doll at East Martello? Who did Carmen Turner replace on the city commission? What was Jimmy Weekley's first mayoral campaign slogan, and what was Shine Forbes' home called?

I didn't say it was a thrill-a-minute, nail-biting, heart-stopping game, but it does pass the time when there's absolutely nothing better to do.

Once you've exhausted the thrill of "thumb wars," have peeled the entire label off your beer bottle without ripping it, and have had the typical conversations with the bartender and other tourists you might be bored enough to start the unnamed Key West trivia game.

I also wouldn't recommend playing the game while sitting home alone watching some god-forsaken M*A*S*H marathon. (Trust me, it's no self-esteem builder.) By the time Hawkeye Pierce starts to lose his mind in Korea, you'll be trying to convince yourself there's a Meredith Avenue somewhere in New Town.

Other questions include naming all the schools from Big Pine south, not counting day care centers. Name seven dive boats and the last names of seven Key West police officers. (Note to you, smug cheaters: Al Flowers is no longer on the force, so he doesn't count in this game.)

What was Simonton's first name? Of course, this one is easier for people who either spend a lot of time in the Pez Garden, ahem, I mean the Historic Memorial Sculpture Garden, or who happen to live somewhere near Simonton Street and hear the Conch Tour Train driver explain the story about how John Simonton bought the island...over and over and over again.

And now, for those of you who have been struggling with the 20 female street names, here's some help: Alberta, Ashby, Caroline, Josephine, Bertha, Virginia, Emma, Elizabeth, Margaret, Olivia. There's at least 10 remaining.

But that's all you're getting from me. I now have better things to do than play this silly little game. My thumbs are recovered and ready for more peanuts, and the theme song to M*A*S*H is relentlessly running through my mind.

September 15, 2002

'TIS THE SEASON

And people say there's no change of season here in the Keys.

I realize most of us haven't been out back stacking firewood, and I'm assuming the market for snow tires is slim.

I wouldn't normally consider subtlety one of Key West's identifying characteristics, but there is an understated shift that takes place each October. People look up at the sky more often. They smile as they take a deep breath upon walking outside.

Autumn has arrived in the Keys and we are no longer sweating.

My air-conditioner has been silent for a week now. Sleeping without its usual background hum took some getting used to, as I now hear everyone traversing Simonton Street between 1 and 4 a.m.

The guy with the Boston accent was convinced the "bahs" in Key West stay open until 4 a.m. and could not understand why the duo was already heading back to the room. His female counterpart disagreed with the closing time, or simply wanted her inebriated beau to curtail his alcohol intake.

The owner of the dog with the aggravating bell on its collar shuffled around outside for at least 15 minutes the other night while cooing to the mangy hound. And the woman locked out of the guesthouse across the street decided to use her God-given talent of whistling through two fingers to get the attention of her friends or the management.

The gentle breeze and open windows that allowed these little tidbits of late-night life into my home, also brought the sweet scent of jasmine and the smug realization that although summer has ended here, the leaves won't fall off the trees, the ground won't freeze and the landscape will never have that bleak February desperation.

I also wore socks a few times this week, and pantyhose.

The pantyhose were part of the Fantasy Fest outfit, and the control top aspect was essential, but the socks were a refreshing accessory.

I dug through the small drawer reserved for them and found a match to accompany a pair of hiking boots.

Yep, the weather has changed and a new season is in the air, but other things are there as well.

The hum of powerboats reverberated over the harbor and around Fort Zach, while an unending compilation of Jimmy Buffett music spills from countless bars. Ah, the sounds of fall in the Keys.

The seasons have changed and 'season' has arrived.

I, for one, am still finding Fantasy Fest beads under the couch and the hangover is too recent to forget. But powerboats have throttled in, and people in stupid hats are wandering around town spelling everything with a "ph." (It's the annual Parrothead convention of people who seem to know more about Jimmy Buffett than he does.)

While the onslaught of out-of-towners might take some of us by surprise every year, it is important to remember their crucial role. Sure, parking is at a premium and the folks in the station wagon with Vermont tags have not yet realized that Olivia is a one-way street. But once they finally park and get out of that station wagon, they will be sleeping in our hotels, drinking in our bars and ordering off our menus.

I know, they're the same people who drink 190 Octanes at Fat Tuesday until they throw up and stare open-mouthed at homosexual couples.

But they will be buying our newspapers, tipping our cab drivers and paying our admission prices.

Our sentiments may be mixed about the loud powerboats and even louder Hawaiian shirts, but both are relatively harmless and absolutely profitable. And besides, most of those people will be stacking firewood in a few months.

November 4, 2001

Think about it:
Key West has an average, year-round temperature of 77 degrees, according to the mayor's letterhead.

PAIN IN THE...

The old jingle for Band-Aids was running through my head the other day as I affixed one of them to my toe.

"I am stuck on Band-Aid, 'cause Band-Aid's stuck on me," replayed itself while I sat hunched over my left foot and still angry with the bed that had caused me such pain.

The bed with all of its metal wheels has been in the same place for a year now, and it was pretty much my own stupidity that caused the high-speed collision between metal and flesh. But it was the bed that received a severe pummeling as I collapsed onto its corner, cradling my foot with one hand and delivering several enraged blows to the mattress.

The little injuries we inflict on ourselves almost daily seem all the more painful because there's no one to blame but ourselves – and the inanimate objects we run into.

The half-empty box of Band-Aids on the coffee table got me thinking about the myriad other universally painful mishaps, such as...

Jamming your toothbrush down into your lower gum line when it slips from your molars. Haven't we brushed our teeth enough to have mastered it by now?

Biting the inside of your cheek while enjoying an exquisite bite of medium-rare steak placed perfectly on the fork with a sautéed onion. This little injury isn't easily hidden and you usually end up squinting in pain and laying your hand on your cheek while your mouth hangs open revealing the half-chewed bite. The second after the accident, you usually realize that the only beverage in front of you is red wine, which will only exacerbate the pain.

Burning that little flap of skin behind your two front teeth when taking that first, premature bite of pizza thereby ruining your enjoyment of the rest of the slice.

Stubbing your little toe on the bed corner or table leg. Notice this only happens when you're barefoot, and usually in the morning so that extreme pain is the first sensory perception your body recognizes in a day that's already been tainted.

Bending a fingernail backward in one of those freak accidents that's over in a fraction of a second. The nail is back into position with a quick flick of your wrist when the thumb snaps it back into place, but the lingering pain still makes your heart race and your whole body tense up.

Sunburn on the top of your feet. It also seems to be the area of sunburn people notice and feel obligated to point out to others. They look down at your glowing feet, shake their head and tsk, tsk, as if feeling sorry for your feet for having the misfortune of being attached to an idiot such as yourself.

The agony of an eyelash under a contact lens. The smallest piece of hair suddenly feels like a white-hot, ballpoint pen being shoved mercilessly into your iris. For your convenience, this little form of misery usually happens while driving in heavy traffic in bright sunlight, so you have to remove your sunglasses to rub your eye thereby blinding your other eye in the sun and jeopardizing fellow motorists.

The tiny burns that come from (a) seatbelt fasteners that have been baking in the sun all day, and (b) the inside snaps or buttons on jeans that just came out of a dryer set on high heat.

Eating enough Cap'n Crunch to tear up the roof of your mouth. You finish one bowl and notice the surplus milk, so you pour some more cereal, but then realize there's not enough milk to cover the additional cereal, so you add more milk. All of a sudden, the box is half empty, you've been staring at the maze on the back of it for 25 minutes and you're drinking ice water to alleviate the pain on the roof of your mouth that is coated with some sort of artificial flavoring.

Getting a few grains of sand in a blister.

Shaving over sunburn.

And that pesky zipper threat guys face on a daily basis.

"I am stuck on Band-Aid..."

March 24, 2002

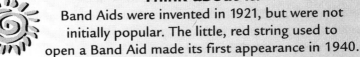

Think about it:
Band Aids were invented in 1921, but were not initially popular. The little, red string used to open a Band Aid made its first appearance in 1940.

A DIRTY JOB, BUT...

Some days are trickier than others in this business of local news.

At times there are too many events, traffic accidents, drug busts, government meetings, whale strandings, suspicious deals and heart-warming tales happening at once to be able to cover them all in the eight, 10 or 12 pages we have.

But at other times nothing happens. Oh sure, the same dirtbag gets arrested for drinking in Bayview Park by the same officer. The same board meets and discusses the same topics without making a decision and the same agency sponsors some type of dinner featuring live entertainment and a silent auction.

Never knowing what is going to be thrown my way on any given day is what makes the job interesting. Unfortunately, finding out what is being thrown often is not.

I would rather whittle away at an infected hangnail than attend some of the meetings I've endured. And I'll never understand why some things just have to happen around 8:30 on a Friday just as I've ordered a cocktail and appetizer.

And there's the phenomenon that dictates that those who think they're newsworthy usually aren't, while the ones who try their best to stay out of print, are the ones who should really be investigated – either for being extraordinarily interesting or amazingly corrupt.

And I can't overlook the countless adventures this job has provided. I've slogged through calf-deep mud to identify homeless encampments and spent Saturday mornings bowling with Special Olympic athletes. I had a bird's eye view of the world's longest rainbow flag being unfurled brilliantly along Duval Street and stoically suffered through some decadent parties overflowing with top-shelf liquor and countless delicacies in puff pastries and rich sauces. Yeah, those are the toughest. I don't know how I get up in the morning.

And then there are the events I have been asked to participate in rather than write about. I have been asked to judge two Mr. Pridefest pageants – the ones that feature men dressed as men on stage at Bourbon Street Pub. Talk about being the token straight female. I was asked to judge a Sloppy Joe's toga party, a drag queen pageant and a rum-mixing contest among local bartenders.

As I said, some days are trickier than others. And I really don't know how I got up the morning of the rum contest. I like being a judge. And I'm not deluding myself into thinking people ask me to judge for my impeccable taste or eye for talent, but because they're hoping for some ink. I'm OK with that, and they're OK with the fact that there are no guarantees.

In fact, while many of you are reading this, I will be at yet another event demonstrating my discriminating palate as I sip a plethora of daiquiris made with Panama Jack Spiced Rum at the Sands Beach Club. Local professionals will be combing the rum with other flavorful medleys and asking a panel of esteemed judges to choose their favorite frozen concoction. I know, I'm getting a little out of control with the "esteemed" bit, but I will be sitting there with the county's Supervisor of Elections Harry Sawyer and I plan to vote often at today's rum-soaked election. Hey, if "esteemed" city leaders can get up close and personal while judging the annual homemade bikini contest at Hog's Breath, then I can have a daiquiri or nine. So if you're in the area this afternoon, stop by the Sands around 3 p.m. to see how the competition heats up and how the judges respond to the pressure.

Oh, and they're giving out free samples.

Let's see how you do getting up in the morning.

October 12, 2003

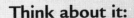

Think about it:

The familiar green Mile Marker signs along U.S. 1 in the Florida Keys begin at Mile Marker 127 south of Florida City. The originals were installed along the old railroad route.

DECEMBER DECISIONS

Have you ever noticed the subtle but distinct division of labor around the holidays?

Certain tasks are reserved for certain people. At least that's how it was Wednesday night at the Monroe Association for Retarded Citizens Christmas tree lot, where I spent a few volunteer hours selling trees, restocking the lot and figuring out how much a hanging poinsettia cost.

I was there with several good-hearted friends who didn't mind lifting hundreds of fir trees and spinning them around to identify any bare spots that would have to face the wall. Fortunately, two of them were also able to operate a chainsaw rather handily, and were there to slice the bottom inch and lowest branches off the trunk.

But one thing we all noticed about the tree decision? Dads, husbands and boyfriends have no say in the selection of the proper tree. (Gay men are no different, so don't go feeling like you're above all this, guys. Admit it, one of you has the final say, while the other eventually bows their head in defeat.)

Sure, the women nod their heads, pretend to listen, show some acknowledgement of height restrictions and then promptly jettison the male opinion from their mind while wandering to the next tree.

Sorry, guys, I'm speaking from both childhood memories and practical experience gained on Southard Street the other night.

One man walked brazenly onto the lot swearing up and down they were not going to have a tree as big as the one they had last year. He was adamant. His head was shaking, even as his wife was standing back to analyze an 11-foot tree that two of us volunteers had lifted and spun.

His refusal was completely muffled by her appraisal of how low the bottom branches were and how many inches had to be cut from the top limb in order to make room for the star. His position was not at all helped by their two boys, who were in complete support of their mother and the enormous tree.

As two of us hefted the thing toward the chainsaw, the wife and mother watched in satisfaction, still deciding which side needed to face the wall, and reminding her husband that he had put it too close to the wall last year.

In the meantime, almost imperceptibly, she relinquished control of the situation. The tree was chosen, but now it had to be a) paid for and b) lashed to the roof of an SUV.

All right, boys, your turn. Yep, that tree is filled with sap. I know, it must be really sticky, and oops, those pine needles do tend to aggravate the skin when lodged inside your sleeve. Well, I assumed you would have thought to bring enough rope to secure such a large tree. I never said I wanted a small tree this year, maybe you could borrow some rope. Hot out here? No, actually, I'm quite comfortable. Mmmmm hmmmmm. Now, what about wreaths this year? Should we put one on the front door AND a few on the balcony? I wonder if I should get three of the same, or a few with different decorations on them.

Just keep lashing and sweating, guys. Your presence is in no way required for this next decision, which has been known to last longer than the tree selection. It involves holding up wreaths, adjusting bows and then wandering around to think about the possibilities and placement before making a decision.

Of course, once it's chosen, paid for and carried inside, the task of hanging it properly will again fall to the man, who will also become responsible for securing the tree in its stand, lashing it up and then spinning the correct side toward the wall.

In my family, my dad always strung the lights first amid some grumbling and near disasters involving his short arms and a teetering tree. With the lights strung to mom's satisfaction, dad could sit back with a glass of wine – until it was time to assemble complex gifts with tiny parts and Chinese instructions.

December 8, 2002

Think about it:

The Monroe Association for Retarded Citizens raises money each year by selling Christmas trees. The trees arrive by refrigerated truck from North Carolina.

ABILITY VERSUS ENJOYMENT

I pay bills because I have to. It's not that I'm particularly good at writing the checks every month and making sure my account number appears on the "memo" line.

I send thank-you notes because I'm expected to. Again, not what one would consider a talent, but a duty that comes with growing up in my family.

But what about the things we do simply because we want to? What makes one activity more appealing than others? I'd say our level of enjoyment is in direct proportion to our ability. The kid picked last for every kickball game probably doesn't like kickball.

I enjoy Scrabble because I'm pretty good at it. I shy away from Monopoly because I've never won. Besides, my older brother probably still has $500 bills stashed under the board while convincing me to buy Water Works.

I stay away from pool tables, as I could be the world's worst pool player.

Luckily, I'm very good at lying perfectly still for several hours, so I enjoy the beach, where I also excel at positioning my book so as not to block the sun.

I don't like creating homemade gifts for friends because I'm not good at it.

I went to Utah last winter because I'm a decent skier. As luck would have it, I'm also pretty adept at hot tubs and corkscrews, conveniently located at the mid-mountain condo.

I avoid calculus, because, well, I'm terrible at it, but I can throw a Frisbee the entire length of a beach without hitting the lifeguard stand and can diagram a complex sentence.

The point is, we usually enjoy things we're good at, but I realized on a recent afternoon that bowling is the exception that proves the rule in my life.

I'm not a strong bowler, yet I enjoyed every minute of my recent afternoon at the Fish Bowl in Islamorada.

The obnoxious bowling alley carpet assaulted my eyes as our group of nine entered the building. The thud of a 12-pound ball making contact with the wooden floor, and then "waah, waah, waahing," toward the 10 pins is unmistakable, as is the hollow clatter of those pins when someone (usually not me) manages to knock a few down.

Is it me, or are the rental shoes disturbingly comfortable? The kids too small for shoes padding around in their socks reminded me of second-grade birthday parties during the dawn of the Carvel ice cream cake that always arrived after the bowling-alley pizza, which tasted eerily similar to skating-rink pizza.

My recent bowling experience happened to be for a friend's 30th birthday (don't ask.) We skipped the ice cream cake, ate the requisite pizza and traded soda in paper cups for pitchers of cheap beer.

"I feel like I'm in an episode of 'Roseanne,'" I whispered while selecting a marbleized ball and watching the more knowledgeable patrons hunch over the hand dryers and score tables.

I did manage to knock down a few pins and even managed all of them at once a few times. So what is the acceptable response to a strike? Skilled bowlers give a dignified nod while walking away from their successful release.

I, on the other hand, leap into the air with some sort of yelp that elicits disgusted glances from other lanes. Then again, those people have also learned that twisting their body in absurd directions after releasing the ball will not keep it out of the gutter.

After three games, two pizzas and a few pitchers, I accepted the fact that I probably will never be a gifted bowler. But as long as the shoes are comfortable, and the man at the counter continues to spray them with disinfectant, I'll keep sending that marbleized sphere down the polished lane. But I still won't play Monopoly against my brother.

February 24, 2002

Think about it:
Most bowling that occurred in the early 1800s took place in cellars or basements attached to saloons.

CHANGE THE CHANNEL

It disturbs me that ALF is back on television and is paired with Emmitt Smith for some long distance service. Had our world become so empty that we had to bring back that Alien Life Form from the 80s? What other obscure character will we see next, Kitt the talking car from "Knight Rider?"

It's bad enough that the guy who played Zach Morris on "Saved By the Bell" is now partners with Sipowitz on "NYPD Blue," but ALF? Come on.

And if ALF's not bad enough when talking about commercials that tell you how to dial a telephone, Carrot Top is constantly screaming about being mediocre, or dialing down the middle, one of them.

That guy wasn't funny when he was performing on my college campus in front of 2,500 college students who had consumed so much booze and drugs that the knot in their shoelaces sent them into hysterics.

Now he's older and more annoying, and is the reason I will never "dial down the middle C-A-L-L-A-T-T."

It just won't happen.

But I do want to know what that drug Imitrex does without having to "ask my doctor if it's right for me."

These new drug commercials never tell you what symptoms, diseases or ailments the pills treat. They just tell you to ask your doctor if "the little purple pill is right for you." There could be a lot of pills right for me. As a matter of fact, I've already found some I like better than others, but I wouldn't know whether to even bring up Imitrex with my doctor unless the commercial tells me what it does.

And what about the hair growth pills that warn women not to take the prescriptions, not to touch the pills or handle broken tablets. Whoa. Okay. Point taken. I get it – those little tablets will instantly put hair on my chest and knuckles, along with producing those little tufts that come out of men's ears and nose. I'll stay far away from them, thanks for the heads up.

And the herpes medication commercial that shows a couple white water rafting, because apparently that's what you want to do during a "flare up." Who knew?

And then we have those poor car companies – they just don't get it.

I don't want to hear some sing-songy "And nobody knows it but me" lyric about outdoor life and an escape to nature in a deluxe, fully loaded SUV that probably has one of those DVD players in the backseat and a computer that can order Chinese food while you're driving.

Show me the car, show me the inside of the car and then tell me how much it costs. What good is a car commercial that shows "a professional driver on a closed course?" How often have you had the chance to weave wildly in and out of traffic cones, or serpentine your way up the side of the mountain at breakneck speeds while listening to opera in a car with seat warmers? The traffic cones haven't presented themselves since my driving test, and the mountain? There's some things I should never be allowed to do.

Okay, there were a few decent Volkswagen commercials a year or so ago about people who couldn't believe they were old enough to have kids in the backseat, but the woman who over enunciates the "u" in Jaguar should be run over with one of the new XJ models.

The sight of that little Sprint PCS monkey in a blue bathrobe with a thermometer cracked me up, but I had had enough of the "Dude, you're getting' a Dell" guy. He was arrested in New York City for trying to buy pot, dude.

And has anyone seen the one for Saturn when the guy on a rope swing smacks directly into the "dent resistant" car doors? It's a good one that capitalizes on the human race's tendency to laugh hysterically at someone who falls down or runs into something.

For the most part, television commercials simply provide an opportunity to go to the bathroom during "Law and Order" and refill my soda while rummaging through the refrigerator. Every once in a while there's one worth watching, but ALF, Emmitt and Carrot Top will always be a bathroom break for me.

April 13, 2003

A PACKAGE DEAL

I hurt myself in a freak hair dryer accident last week.

I was not strangled by the cord, and did not decide to save time by bringing the small appliance into the bathtub with me.

The injury occurred as I was wielding scissors and trying to wrestle open the plastic packaging containing my new hair dryer.

The old one finally died in a blaze of small but potent electric shocks and plumes of black smoke that smelled like charred hair – a rather unpleasant morning experience.

My hair dried in the sun and I replaced the electric device with a simple, run-of-the-mill, off-low-med-high speed hair dryer that cost about $15.

The dryer works fine as long as I hold it correctly to avoid contact with the gash in my palm that resulted from the lengthy and profanity-filled task of getting the molded plastic package open.

Are you familiar with the material? It's as if two stiff pieces of clear plastic are heat sealed together after the apparatus has been placed between them. There is no perforated line for easy opening, and no "pull here to open" tab.

So I attacked the packaging with scissors sharper than anything I should be allowed to handle and sliced through the thick plastic, which immediately splintered into two razor sharp points, one of which slid directly into the fleshy part of my hand.

It was just as well, really, because if the packaging hadn't done it, the scissors were bound to.

I don't understand the concept behind this sort of container for items and other similarly impossible packaging strategies.

Remember Capri Sun fruit drinks? Do they still make them, and if so, have them made them any easier to open? Who knows how many times I jammed the pointed end of the little plastic straw through both sides of the odd, foil-like pouch sending a stream of artificially flavored fruit juice into my lap.

And what about the music industry? We evolved away from cassette tapes that came in that hideous plastic scaffolding that had to be run over with a car before it would release the shrink-wrapped cassette.

And we have replaced it with the shrink-wrapped CD that requires the removal of that strip of tape that never comes off in one piece.

Surely there must be some alternatives. There are many, many items that come in convenient, risk-free packaging and dispensers.

I have never hurt myself with a shampoo bottle. It's a rather basic, but quite appropriate dispenser with its flip top, squeezable flexibility and the opportunity to fill it with water and shake in order to get the last of the hair product out of it.

Of course, it has exploded in luggage, but no injuries there.

Toothpaste is pretty safe, and the tube's efficient, but has anyone ever gotten the final drop out?

How about matchbooks? Talk about the perfect combination of form and function. I know, there is some injury risk inherent with matches, but it really is the ideal packaging – until they get wet.

Lipstick is in a good self-contained package, as is nail polish.

I bought cookies and milk the other night and loved the fact that the mini Chips Ahoy came in a resealable bag with a Ziploc-type closure, which is pure genius. I heaved a sigh of relief when I realized we would not be under pressure to eat the entire bag so as to eliminate the risk of the cookies becoming mushy with humidity. (Of course, the resealable bag proved unnecessary later that evening as the last little cookie took a long bath in cold milk.)

The little, black film canisters are pretty nifty, and Scotch tape is convenient, although there is that little sharp cutting edge to be wary of. I don't remember drawing blood after wrapping a gift.

Then again, most people probably don't have to cover their hands with Band-Aids before drying their hair.

March 16, 2003

BE OUR GUESTS

We share this island. We don't always enjoy doing so, but it's part of the responsibility that comes from living where million of others choose to vacation. It's the same in every resort town. And since it's not possible to draw a masking tape line across the island, we'll have to go on living side by side, bumper to bumper with people who don't know that some streets are one-way, who stop in the middle of a crowded sidewalk to gawk at a rooster and who find it amusing that there's actually a high school in Key West.

Cohabitation is possible, if not ideal. But it could be helpful to identify and describe the various categories of visitors. Understanding their instincts may help us better deal with them while driving downtown, or at the very least, may help us avoid their natural habitats.

The Margaritaville tourists are obsessed with Jimmy Buffett. They test each other on the origins of his songs, know his kids' middle names and hope against hope that he'll sit in for a surprise session that night at his bar, otherwise known as Mecca.

They're typically harmless unless present in huge volume during the annual convention of others like themselves. And it's often fun, if a little cruel, to send them into a frenzy by whispering loudly to a friend in the Hog's Breath that you heard Buffett was playing at Margaritaville in about 25 minutes. They look at each other with wide eyes, thrilled with their insider information that came from a local so it has to be true.

Matching T-shirt tourists are often here for a family reunion and feel the need to let everyone know that the Wilsons are here from Topeka in 2002. Often unaccustomed to humidity, the reunion group stands, confused and sweating, on street corners consulting a map and trying to get 14 people to agree on a dinner destination.

They're likely to get seasick on an afternoon snorkel trip and can be seen secretly nudging each other, chuckling about a generic, raunchy T-shirt in any one of the generic, raunchy T-shirt shops. They'll never buy the naughty shirts, but are likely to walk out of the store with a shirt that still smells like the hot iron that attached a decal of a sailboat.

Collegiate tourists boast hotel sinks filled with ice and cans of cheap beer, and are likely to fall in lust with a sun-tanned boat mate who keeps pouring draft beer.

Twosome tourists are either gay or straight couples meandering through Old Town, dining out and drinking heavily.

The straight couples are fun to watch when the woman is walking about three steps in front of her significant other with her arms crossed, and mouth contorted into a petulant frown. The guy is usually bent forward with his arm outstretched begging forgiveness for a mysterious crime he doesn't know he committed.

One of my all-time favorite overheard arguments started with, "Honey, we've only been married two weeks and already you want to go to a strip bar?"

Another came from a man who told his lady friend, "I don't want another beer – I want you to shut up."

Visiting gay couples, on the other hand, boldly hold hands while walking through town. Their eyes dart from one passerby to another as if testing the town's reputation for tolerance. They can't do this on a street in Minnesota, but have heard it's all right to hold hands in Key West, so they do. Some seem almost disappointed when no one cares or even notices.

Cruise ship passengers are quite apparent in their mission to obtain a T-shirt from a Hard Rock Café in every hemisphere. Don't try telling them about Mangoes' yellowtail, the conch chowder at Turtle Kraals or Buddy's fish sandwich. They'll have a cheeseburger at the Hard Rock like they've had in every other port for the past two weeks.

On second thought, about that masking tape line across the island...

June 23, 2002

Think about it:
There are 4,322 legal hotel rooms in Key West.

RUNNING OUT & RUNNING AROUND

There was no ketchup in the refrigerator the other day. This was no emergency, but it was strange because I can't remember a time when there wasn't ketchup in there. Even stranger is that I can't remember buying ketchup – ever.

Ketchup's one of those refrigerator mainstays, sort of like the assortment of salad dressings and other condiments that line themselves up in the door of the refrigerator – small bottles of Tabasco hiding behind the big thing of ranch dressing. It's just always supposed to be there.

But last week I pattied up a burger, flipped it once and tried to create the perfect juxtaposition of ketchup, mustard and pickles. But there was no ketchup left, just a depressing puff of phlegmy air escaping from the bottle as I futilely squeezed.

I hate running out of stuff, but it happens quite often in the chaos that is my life. The ketchup was a recent, but minor, example of my shortsightedness.

It's also resulted in me pawing through the garbage can because I ejected the old cartridge of the Gillette Mach 3 razor into the trash before being sure I had a refill.

Or my lack of forethought becomes apparent in wet footprints that stemmed from my failure to ensure that a towel was in the bathroom before stepping into the shower. I'm always amazed at how much water the surface area of my body collects and how soaked the carpet can actually get no matter how quickly I dash in one fluid movement – like a gazelle – from the bathroom to the bedroom.

Truth be told, I've never done anything remotely gazelle-like, but it's even worse if that mad dash for a towel is transformed into an obstacle course because I have not only run out of towels, but also lightbulbs. The one from the living room is in the bathroom and the one from the bedroom is in the kitchen.

As I run through the living room to the bedroom, I think to myself how I've never seen a gazelle slam into a doorjamb and get its foot tangled in the strings of bikini top. It must be much easier to run through the woods.

Given the fact that I put things in my eyes, adjust temperature dials and use triple-blade razors in the bathroom, it's really best that the last remaining lightbulb ends up there. If there are two left, the other goes to the kitchen. I struggle enough with cooking skills, so I needn't compound the problem by throwing the perplexing room into utter darkness. If no lightbulb is available for that room, I call the nice people at China Garden.

My shortsightedness, which could also be called laziness, or attributed to a physical condition that began in college with a massive die-off of brain cells, also manifests itself in the form of a Walkman or camera that doesn't work because the AA batteries from it are now being used to power the television remote.

Of course, the camera's only missing batteries when there's actually film in it. My camera almost never has both ingredients, and when it does there's nothing worthy of a picture.

I did, however, just fill the container that holds windshield wiper fluid for my car. I was tired of that obnoxious grating sound of wiper against dry windshield, and even more tired of the resulting arc of grime that spreads from one side to the other.

I also got the oil changed in my car. Motor oil is one thing I never run out of. It's apparently somewhat necessary for vehicle operation, and I've chosen not to test its importance. But I still feel a sense of proud accomplishment after having the oil changed and the fluid levels checked.

I can almost hear my car sighing contentedly in appreciation as I hit the gas pedal.

My plants let out a sigh similar when I water them, as do my teeth after flossing.

Dental floss is another one of those things that just always seems to be in the bathroom cabinet. But it poses a unique challenge because you can't always see inside to determine how much is left on the spool.

Such was not the case with the clear, plastic ketchup bottle, and my unevenly adorned burger became like a wet footprint on the living room carpet – at least I could still change the channel in the dark.

SITTIN' PRETTY

Am I the only one who thinks riding side-saddle on a scooter is absurd?

We've all seen those proper few in town who look like they're about to slide off the black vinyl seats and land in a heap on Eaton Street amid a pile of long skirt.

I don't get it, but then, I don't own a scooter. Trust me, it's better this way.

In my last serious bike accident, I got hit by a car – a parked car. It's true, I tore open my forearm and needed 17 stitches using just the force of my own legs. I shudder to think what I could do to myself or others while perched on a motorized machine not surrounded by metal.

I am not unfamiliar with the world of Hondas, Moskitos and the cool, new People scooters. I've borrowed them from friends and rented my own for a few days while my car was in the shop.

And although I spend most of my driving time behind the wheel of a car, I have begun to take notice of the subtle, yet telling, variations of the scooter world.

Take, for example, posture. There is an amazing number of ways to sit on a scooter. Think about the folks we see on North Roosevelt Boulevard, or the ones inching out at an Old Town intersection.

There are those who sit up very straight and ride with their feet and knees together on the floorboard. Their eyes are glued to the road in front of them (not that there's anything wrong with that) and not even the sight of the mayor in high heels and a leather miniskirt would get their attention.

Then there are the slightly more comfortable-looking riders who sit in a relaxed slouch with their feet slightly apart, eyes taking in everything around them, including oncoming traffic and careless drivers, but also the mayor in his high heels and miniskirt and the bartender who bought the first round last night.

But the most striking of scooter postures is the heart-stopping wobble of a sunburned novice. Their shoulders are hunched into their neck, their elbows stick far out to the side and their blinker is always on. They resemble an adolescent llama, lanky, and still trying to move smoothly. (No, I have never seen an adolescent llama, but I'd imagine they're rather knock-kneed and awkward.)

The novices careen a bit while venturing into an intersection and bump their feet along the pavement a few times before remembering to lift them up and place them on the floorboard provided. But they never remember to turn off the blinker.

There are other varying traits of scooter operators perhaps not immediately recognizable to the untrained eye, but have you ever noticed that some people put only one foot on the ground while stopped at red light? They lean on one leg, hitching up the opposite hip while keeping the other foot on the floorboard. Others stop with both feet on the ground, often standing up to pull the leg of their shorts down.

Some people look behind them when stopped at red light to see if they know the driver of the car, who if anything like me at a red light, is staring at them. Others steadfastly refuse to look around and see who is studying them.

Oh, and let us not forger the two straight-guys-on-a-scooter phenomenon.

The guys, through some unfortunate turn of events in their evening, ended up having to share a scooter on the way back to their hotel. After a brief struggle over who's going to drive, the two position themselves as far from each other as possible while still remaining, barely, on the seat.

The guy in the rear would just as soon slide off the back of the seat than hold onto the driver, who leans as far forward as possible, as if trying to increase the aerodynamics of the vehicle. They end up looking as ridiculous the women riding side-saddle and are just as likely to end up in a heap on Eaton Street.

April 21, 2002

Think about it:
The city of Key West operates 822 parking meters.

THE PRICE OF FEAR

Fear is a funny thing. Many of us are willing to pay insane amounts of money to be genuinely afraid. We enjoy it, we call it a rush, and it's addictive.

Take roller coasters, for example. Amusement parks are a huge industry in the United States and all over the world. Sure, we're aware of what's basically going to happen once we're strapped in, but we don't know exactly when that moment of descent will come as the car reaches the precipice of that huge climb, sending our stomach into our ribcage.

If you think about it, there really is no guarantee that the car will stay on the track, that the track will support the weight of the cars, our bodies and that of the immeasurably fat guy up front who can barely get that shoulder harness around him.

We're also never sure that the shoulder harness will remain locked in place while we're twirled around metal loops that make a distinct clicking sound as the car passes it.

Perhaps the rush comes from the proximity to danger. We willingly pay $50 to get into some "amusement" parks and then wait in lines for up to an hour simply to have the bejeezus scared out of us for all of two and a half minutes.

In college I paid something like $200 (twice) to hurl myself out of a perfectly good airplane and fall 13,500 feet back to the North Carolina ground. Again, I was pretty sure the parachute would open but the possibility that it wouldn't made me drunk with adrenaline.

If everything were guaranteed safe and there were no risks to be encountered, very few things would excite or scare us.

There is very little risk associated with going to the movies, yet we pay $8 to grip the arms of our chairs, scrunch down in our seats and watch some horrifying scene of human suffering between our fingers that try unsuccessfully to cover our eyes for two hours.

But the fear from a scary movie often lasts longer than two hours and reminds us that, while the chances are slim, there could very well be a madman on the loose stalking us. Again, proximity to danger.

The fear from a scary movie, and I'm talking about suspenseful scary, not stupid and gory, stays with us. It follows us into the dark parking lot, where our backseat has never looked more ominous. We suddenly realize that any average, run-of-the-mill psychopath can get into the backseat through the unlocked trunk – or the unlocked doors, for that matter.

The residual movie fear continues at home as we become convinced someone is in the house and hiding behind the shower curtain. Yep, $8 well spent, still scared and now having to pay a more costly energy bill as the kitchen light is left on while I sleep.

I had to stop reading Stephen King's "The Shining" one summer because of how frantically my mind was working even after I put the book down. I was in a 100-year-old guesthouse that creaked when you stepped on certain boards. Keep in mind that was the only similarity to the creepy house in the book since mine was a beach house, in the summertime, in a crowded resort town. Oh, and my dad rarely used an axe to chop through doors.

We'll pay to be scared and to put ourselves into harm's way. So why did I not enjoy, not one bit, the paralyzing dread that came as a scorpion stalked across the bathroom floor? I didn't get that euphoric rush as the thing then disappeared temporarily under the claw foot tub. I wouldn't have paid $8 for that feeling, nor for that panicked irrational feeling that flew in with the freakishly large moth, prompting me to flail wildly with a broom to the detriment of the ceiling fan. Nope, not worth $8.

Why do we relish some fears and dread others? I suppose it's because on some level, we actually do know that there's no freak in a hockey mask in the bathroom and chances are minuscule that the roller coaster will collapse. But when it comes to giant moths, there just are no guarantees. The thing had murder in its eyes, and was trying to communicate with its scorpion buddy in the bathroom. I swear they were both wearing hockey masks.

July 20, 2003

"COMPLIMENTARY" GIFTS

The woman at the front desk smiled and seemed sincere when she thanked me for staying there and hoped I had enjoyed my stay. I signed the itemized bill and handed over the encoded key cards.

Little did she know that even though I had willingly signed off on a $13 hotel breakfast that consisted of a cold English muffin, one egg of some sort and barely cooked hashbrowns, I had a few things of hers tucked away in my bag.

Of course, they didn't really belong to the woman at the desk, and she'll never miss them.

But a place that charges $13 for a crappy breakfast – and threatens to charge $4.50 for a packet of Oreos in the mini-bar – deserves to lose a few bottles of "complimentary" shampoo, conditioner and body lotion along with those wonderful little sewing kits that come with two buttons for Oxford shirts and those dainty, gold safety pins. Oh, I also took the tiny Heinz ketchup jar that came with breakfast. It's really quite adorable.

I left the complimentary shower cap in the bathroom, but made sure the room was cleared of matches, pens and little notepads with the hotel's logo at the top. The hotel obviously wants me to have it, otherwise they wouldn't have left them strewn about.

I know I'm not alone in these episodes of pilferage. We just can't resist those little toiletry items. So what if we'll never, ever use them – they're free and are apparently unlimited because housekeepers replace them every day. These ladies aren't stupid. I know they notice my Pantene shampoo in the shower, and also notice that the entire assortment of bathroom items is gone – except for the shower cap.

Yet tirelessly they replace the little bottles and tubes and sewing kits and matches after changing the sheets and folding my clothes.

So why do we feel the need to check out with more than our share of mini things? Why do some of us, who shall remain nameless, insist on peering through the peephole waiting for the housekeeping employee to leave her cart unattended and therefore vulnerable?

Why do we do this?

How many times, in a year, do you find yourself using that little tube of conditioner with the Hyatt logo on the cap? And don't give me the "they come in handy on business trips" response because when you're on a business trip, you're in another hotel, in another city, with similar shampoo supplies.

I'll admit, I currently have about nine little bottles in my medicine cabinet and three sewing kits, all of which are missing the buttons, safety pins and most of the white and blue thread. I don't have any shower caps.

But I don't steal towels – or the in-room coffee makers.

I do remember hearing of a hotel that actually had a sign with a price list in the bathroom acknowledging the popularity of their towels, and letting guests know how much they would charge the guest's credit card for each missing washcloth and bath towel.

My friends and family being who they are – stole the sign.

On the recent trip to Fort Lauderdale, our room was also missing the Bible when we checked out. It wasn't me. I kept thinking lightning was going to strike us down, or at least strike at the one who actually took it and hit me instead. Nothing happened, apparently those Gideons are OK with it.

I enjoy the pleasant anonymity of hotels, and the fact that someone comes in every morning to clean up. I like the clean and folded towels and the way the end of the roll of toilet paper is always folded into a point. I like walking down the hallway in my socks at nighttime to fill my ice bucket, and, on the way check out what other people ordered from room service based on the leftover scraps they put outside their door.

And I like the complimentary continental breakfasts some places provide. But it's a little tougher to sneak a handful of complimentary apple danishes into your bag. And if the lady at the front desk catches you, she could also make you give back the shampoo.

June 22, 2003

PEOPLE WHO...

Did you ever stop to think about the personality traits that bug you? They're insignificant little details that seem trivial at first, but begin to bother us exponentially, like a mosquito bite you want to scratch until it bleeds.

For instance, I can't stand...

• People who only eat the cashews out of a bowl of mixed nuts. It's perfectly acceptable to prefer cashews over peanuts, almonds, pecans and macadamias. It's even all right to eyeball the bowl before taking a handful to locate a particular cluster of cashews. But don't pick one by one, it's narrow-minded.

• People who shake your hand at a gathering and say, "It's nice to meet you," when they know full well they've met you at least twice before in similar situations.

Is it so hard to say, "Nice to see you again," or "Oh, hi, where did we last see each other?"

No, instead some people have to take the condescending approach that implies they have met and remembered the names of so many other, more important, people, they can't be bothered with yours. It makes that person seem arrogant and leaves me hoping they step in dog excrement just before their next high-society function.

• People with vanity license plates that have no obvious meaning for fellow motorists. Let's face it, these people don't get the obnoxious tags for themselves – they rarely see them. These frivolous little expenditures should at least have some meaning for the people who actually read them.

And while we're on the subject, the same people who continually tell you how nice it is to meet you are often guilty of having cocky vanity plates like the one I saw in my hometown years ago that read, PD CASH." It was on some sort of red convertible. At least it made sense while telling the world what a yutz the guy was.

• People (usually women) who enter a party complaining about how terrible their hair looks, or how their outfit makes them look fat..

C'mon ladies, if something makes us look worse than we think we deserve, we change. A comment like "Oh my God, these pants make my butt look huge," is only proffered as a request for a counter compliment like, "Oh, stop, you look fantastic."

• People (usually men) who find it necessary to turn down the car radio while looking for a street sign or address. Most people (still usually men) guilty of this act cite that they cannot concentrate with the music on. I just don't know what looking for an address has to do with hearing the radio – perhaps I'll never know.

Then again, I'll admit to having intentionally driven past my destination with the radio blaring simply because I like the song that just came on. A few trips around the block is always worth a few minutes of a treasured '80s love song that appeared on countless homemade "mix" tapes.

• People who stand up immediately after the airplane stops. OK folks, the seatbelt sign was turned off so it's time to turn down the corner of the page of your book, shove it into your backpack – and wait.

Wait through the tinkling cacophony of 200 seatbelt releases. Wait for the flight crew to "prepare the cabin for cross check and arrival," whatever that is, although it seems to take an inordinate amount of time before people actually begin to progress up the aisle and out of the aircraft.

Everyone stands up immediately, necks bent an unnatural angles under the call button, jockeying for position near what has suddenly become "their" overhead compartment.

Relax, sit down. Have a cashew and tell me about your license plate.

January 13, 2002

Think about it:
The cashew tree is related to American poison ivy and poison sumac. The nut is related to both the pistachio and the mango.

71

TAKE NOTE

The Post-it note on the side of my computer monitor has been reminding me to do something for the past seven weeks. I must look at it 40 times a day, yet have no idea what it says.

The little, yellow square has been there for so long the adhesive is barely effective and although I have to reattach it regularly with tape, its message remains a mystery.

On the other hand, I have a vivid mental picture of the phone number and flight confirmation number I scribbled on the back of an envelope just before accidentally throwing the envelope away with a bunch of credit card offers, which was right before I scraped two plates of pasta and some Caesar salad into the trashcan.

Why is it that the items we purposefully make note of and take pains to post in a conspicuous spot tend to get ignored and overlooked, but the stuff of vital importance – flight times, account numbers and directions to an afternoon job interview – end up, without fail, on napkins, paper plates, the back of receipts and deposit slips and jammed into the margin of the phone book?

I blame this little inevitability, partly, on the advent of the cordless phone. Not cellular phones, necessarily, but the cordless phones that invaded households in the 80s.

Sure, they gave people the freedom to move around, but it took them away from the little note pad that was always next to the kitchen telephone. The pad might still be there because old habits die hard, but if most houses are anything like mine, then the cordless phone is rarely on its charger and a person therefore could be anywhere in the house trying to write down someone's new phone number. The laundry room, for instance, is a particularly tough spot to find a pen and paper.

And just as the most important scribblings tend to get lost, crumpled or covered with spaghetti, why is that useless little scraps such as last week's grocery list miraculously survive a ride in the washer and dryer, but the scrap we might actually need ends up, mockingly, in the lint filter?

But moving on from the little scraps of paper that tend to contribute to the chaos in our pockets, purses, wallets and lives, let's look at the larger-than-life instrument for jotting important and official look-ing notes or lists – the lined, yellow, legal pad.

It looks so regal with its blue lines and red margin, but often con-tains the same type of scribblings and notations as Post-it notes. The only difference is that these legal pads are accepted at board meetings worldwide, so as the guy next to you seems to be diligently jotting down every word of the inane Power Point presentation that's lulling you to sleep, look over his shoulder and see if he isn't just making a to-do list for the weekend.

Of course, legal pads are better suited for longer, more detailed to-do lists. Plus, we'd all look a little silly scribbling furiously on tiny squares of paper and then peeling them away and plastering them all over the conference table during a board meeting.

But I do have a problem with legal pads – why must they be so tall? I realize they are "legal" sized, but haven't the "lawyers" noticed that the rest of the world has pretty much embraced the size and design of the 8 1/2" x 11" piece of paper?

How long until they realize that the yellow pads are really an awkward size? They don't fit inside most file folders and screw up the size uniformity in any stack of papers, documents and folders.

But there remains a certain thrill that comes from crossing every-thing off a to-do list that was written, usually in black ink, all caps, on a legal pad.

It makes the tasks seem more important so completing them makes us feel more accomplished, unless you're like me and tend to add trivial tasks to such lists.

The obvious chores, like brushing your teeth and eating lunch, need not be written down, but they present an opportunity to cross things off, and the more horizontal lines of completion, the better.

Of course, an added benefit of Post-it notes is the ease with which they crumble and are discarded upon completion.

PLAYERS ON A STAGE

photo: roboneal.com

Ever notice how our lives become part of a show that unfolds itself to tourists?

Last week, two cruise ship passengers passed my house as I was taking out the garbage.

"Oh, look, tomorrow must be garbage day in this neighborhood," the man said, genuinely fascinated.

I'm quite sure they were cruise ship passengers, but am still wondering how they found a street other than Duval or Front. The requisite plastic sun visors shaded their eyes. Margaritaville shopping bags hung from their forearms.

Their clothes, bright but ill-fitting and crumpled by perspiration, were obviously bought expressly for their vacation – along with the strappy sandals the woman thought looked tropical in Illinois, but were, by the time she reached Simonton Street, turning her feet into a mottled, blistering mess.

They would end up with T-shirts from Key West, Cozumel and the Bahamas, along with a few from a Hard Rock Café thrown in for good measure. They would come back, barely tanned, but regaling their friends with tales of the heat and swearing that by the end of the trip their blood had thinned enough to tolerate it.

"Man, Key West used to be so hip," a good friend said, shaking his head in disgust the other afternoon as we were forced to brave the melee that is Front and Whitehead street when one or more ships are in port.

He looked at the throngs of people blindly following shore excursion representatives. Like lemmings racing to their death at the edge of a cliff, they followed anyone holding a sign. To make matters worse, some were following a grown woman taking herself way too seriously considering she was holding cardboard Mickey Mouse ears high above her head expecting people to follow, and they did.

Don't get me wrong, I realize the city makes needed money by allowing the behemoth ships to release thousands of people into a four-block area, but is it all really worth it? And if we do need the money, then raise the fees. Double them. We'd have fewer ships and the same revenue.

Just a suggestion, but I've gotten off my topic and onto a soapbox.

The other day, a trio on the Conch Tour Train watched with

disturbing intensity as I crossed Simonton Street heading for a stuffed pork chop at Fausto's deli counter. A friend was stopped at the nearby traffic light, so a sidewalk-to-stoplight conversation took place about my pork chop, activities of the previous night and plans for the upcoming evening.

The conversation was an innocuous exchange that takes place hundreds of times a day. But you would have thought I was telling my friend how I had just chopped up my transsexual grandmother and stuffed her in the Dumpster behind the Chinese restaurant, all while listening to Jimmy Buffett music.

These people were enthralled by pork chops and happy hour plans. I couldn't believe it. Wasn't there a couple fighting somewhere in public? Was there no drag queen standing in front of a bar with an eye-catching outfit and impossible heels? That's something to see. Where was the guy who paints himself silver and stands like a statue awaiting tips?

But all of a sudden my plans had taken on great significance. I may have rethought the pork chop selection had I known a few complete strangers would be entering it in their travel journals.

As the train turned at the light, instead of listening to the driver explain the history and benefits of eyebrow houses and their architecture, the passengers were mesmerized by a woman feeding three cats.

I'll be taking the garbage out again Wednesday night if anyone wants to get to the show early. And on Saturdays? I water the plants. Maybe the woman with the mouse ears will lead her sunburned masses to my house.

March 2, 2003

I PLEDGE ALLEGIANCE

photo: roboneal.com

I have written about the history of the rainbow during gay pride week, and have taken a giant stride off the back of a boat boasting a "diver down" flag.

But I had not said the Pledge of Allegiance in nearly a decade.

Back then it was as much a part of my morning ritual as the altered taste of orange juice after toothpaste.

Nestled between the Our Father and morning announcements over the PA system, the Pledge was recited haltingly, three words at a time by a group of students who limply placed their hands over their heart and worried about the test next period.

I said those 31 words last week, listened to myself and realized the strength of this country and the power of allegiance.

It has erupted in Key West and all over the nation. American flags now fly at half-staff where dive flags once distinguished the dive shops, and where rainbows pointed to guesthouses.

People not normally gifted in the realm of arts and crafts have been using hot glue guns to attach tiny safety pins to red, white and blue ribbons. "God Bless America" has been replaying itself in people's minds. Stores on Duval Street are selling out of everything with the stars and stripes on it and people who have abhorred bumper stickers since they learned to drive have affixed decals to their bumpers and taped flags to their windows.

In this time of renewed patriotism, it also seems that allegiance may have temporarily replaced tourism in the southernmost city. We have loads of American flags, but few people are jumping off dive boats, or staying in guesthouses.

Tour trains are eerily vacant. Parking is plentiful. And vendors are panicked, mentally calculating each day's net losses and wondering how long people will stay away.

But the answer is not clear and no formula can be applied to decipher how long a nation needs to heal.

The Novocaine has worn off. We are no longer numb, and are ready to move ahead nationally and personally. But the wound is still deep and moving ahead does not always mean vacations, sunshine and barhopping.

It could mean New Yorkers returning to work, Californians turning off the televisions that have been bringing the opposite coast into their living rooms.

For some it might just mean raising the flag in front of their Tennessee home to its proper height.

There is no telling how long Key West's streets will be a little emptier, but the spirit of the town has not been vacated.

Look at the listings of events created to help the rescue workers in New York. Restaurants, bars, bands and boats are teaming up to help even with rents due in a week.

Boat captains are donating their time for a nighttime cruise. Waitstaff are donating their precious tips to the cause, firemen are lining the hot streets to fill their boots, school children are writing letters to police officers and firefighters, drag queens are passing the bucket during one song each night for the victims of the terrorism, and guests at dinner parties are passing hats that quickly fill with checks made out to the American Red Cross.

Hotel occupancy is down, but the town is not out, not by a long stretch.

This town cannot be divided by quiet bars and empty hotels. It can be united through help, compassion and the cooperation that makes this place home. As we pass the American flags that line the streets and hang from balconies, remember the words of the Pledge of Allegiance as they pertain to the nation and to our island – "indivisible, with liberty and justice for all."

I don't remember learning the Pledge of Allegiance. I don't remember memorizing it. I don't remember the first time I heard it, or the name of the person who wrote it.

I'm just glad I remembered it, and in the wake of all that has happened, I will never again forget.

September 23, 2001

DRY IDEA

I miss paper towels.

Was there really something so seriously wrong with them that almost every public restroom in America was forced to switch to hand dryers?

If the things actually worked don't you think we would have started putting them in our homes? It would save laundry time with the hand towels. It would cut in half the number of times the little bathroom wastebasket has to be emptied. And if you pointed it toward the mirror after the shower, it would get rid of the fog.

So why aren't we embracing this amazing little contraption? Because it doesn't work.

Have you ever actually stood there, in the bathroom, "wringing your hands together briskly" (as the instructions say) until they were completely dry? You'd be there about seven minutes.

Instead, everyone gives it a few seconds and then walks out of the restroom wiping their hands on their jeans.

Of course, I can only speak knowledgeably about women's public restrooms. Guys' bathrooms are a bit of a mystery (unless the line is too long at the ladies room and some nice guy promises to watch the door while he lets you into the men's room.)

Besides, I'm quite convinced guys skip the hand-washing step when no one else is in the bathroom.

But hand dryers aren't the only disadvantages to the necessary evil that is public restrooms. They're not the cleanest, most fresh-scented or comfortable places in the world, but we all need them at some point, having grown quite accustomed to the miracles of indoor plumbing and flush toilets.

We all need them unless, of course, you are my mother, who, I believe, has survived more than 50 years without ever using one.

She gets this distinctive wrinkle of disgust between her eyebrows when she scrunches up her whole face as someone in the family announces they have to use the bathroom at the next gas station on the highway.

Amazingly, my mom also had the ability to know the exact

capacity of her children's (and husband's) bladders. She could tell us, in no uncertain terms, that we in fact did not need to use the facilities, but rather could wait another 80 miles or so until we reached our destination.

But when the essence of the emergency is at last revealed, and the driver concedes to pull over at some God-forsaken gas station that still sells Tab sodas and has not yet upgraded their gas pumps to the digital display, my mom goes into convulsions just looking at the outside of the building.

She still warns us (although we're all grown adults, who manage to travel alone throughout the world and use the bathroom successfully in each destination) not to touch anything and to wash our hands thoroughly.

It's best not to point out to my mother that in most of these establishments, soap is not an option in the restroom. But since she has never entered one, she'll be none the wiser.

But one thing that does baffle me is the key situation at such facilities.

Must every key be attached to a broomstick or piece of PVC pipe as long as my arm? I realize the point is to keep people from stealing said key, but who would want unlimited access to such a horrid little room?

And what is it about psychology that prevents people from flushing a public toilet? Most of the time you can flush with your foot so your skin doesn't have to touch any surface (not the skin on your hand, at least.)

And while we're on that subject, did anyone else grow up in a family whose mother insisted on laying strips of toilet paper on the seat just before allowing you, as a tiny child, to sit down? And even then she'd get that wrinkled, scrunched up look and be constantly telling you that you could have waited until you got home.

Adulthood has brought with it certain freedoms, one of which includes being able to judge for myself how full my bladder is, although my mother still doesn't believe me. And she still rolls her eyes when she sees me drying my hands on my jeans.

February 2, 2003

photo: roboneal.com

That's it. I've changed my mind. Make it stop.

I was their biggest defender, a bastion of acceptance and hospitality, happy to survive a couple noisy nights so others could have a good time here.

But this is out of control. Yes, they tip well, and most are rather pleasant to talk to. Their T-shirts have hysterical sayings on the backs of them, and the combination of steel and chrome is beautiful.

But last night (early this morning, actually) I woke up convinced someone had driven a Harley into my living room. Wednesday night I dreamt I was at a race track in North Carolina – the sound outside had become the soundtrack for my slumber as 15 bikers became trapped between two red lights in front of my house.

Not only did I get to hear each and every unit of horsepower thundering in anticipation of the green light, but I also got to hear a 45-second conversation being screamed from one seat to the next. They had already been to Sloppy Joe's, but were going back anyway, and yes, they were going in the right direction, but there was no (expletive) way they were going back to the room yet, and they would park in the same (expletive) area they parked last night.

Have these people not yet realized that they wouldn't have to yell if they would just stop revving their engines during the conversation?

But wait, let's clarify some things before there actually is a Harley being driven angrily through my bedroom.

I am not part of the anti-biker, anti-noise, anti-amplified music, anti-everything contingent in Old Town who realizes a little too late that things tend to get noisy in a commercial district, and all whining will be drowned out by music.

It's like the folks who bought a home near the airport last year and are surprised their backyard is a little noisy.

(Disclaimer: For the minority of people in Old Town who have lived there for more than 25 years and have watched the commerce grow up around the area, the above statement does not apply to you.)

I love my downtown neighborhood and everything that comes with it. We get couples fighting. We hear the occasional homeless brawl, bottles breaking, cat fights involving sounds that seem impossible for the little animals to make, guests locked out of nearby guesthouses screaming into a cell phone, music from the bars a block away, police sirens and screaming fire engines.

But again, this week has been out of control.

This is not the Poker Run. These visitors are part of the overflow crowd from Daytona's Bike Week. They are not here for the sanctioned, charity event and therefore have no idea how controversial the issue of motorcycle noise is and has been in this town.

Poker Run participants are bombarded with reminders about unacceptable noise levels and warnings about illegal straight pipes, and I have never wished they would go away.

I like wandering, albeit delicately, past the precisely leaning lines of motorcycles on Duval Street. I've interviewed Poker Run riders and organizers and once got approval from a former boyfriend to select a Harley, find the corresponding driver and ask for a short ride through town.

"Just make sure you pick someone who'll bring you back," he said. "I'm not going to be the one to tell your dad you disappeared on the back of a Harley."

Those were the days. But as of this week I have jumped ship, changed sides, turned coat, missed out on snippets of conversation, lost hours of sleep and gone deaf.

Remember the good old days when the only thing we complained about in March was the relentless drone of scooter horns? So far the bikes have drowned out the mosquito-like buzz. I never thought I'd miss that sweet, collegiate sound.

March 10, 2002

Think about it:
2003 marked Harley-Davidson's 100th birthday.

THE THINGS WE DO

A friend of mine hides money from himself. He makes a few deposits into an account he never accesses, or throws a few $20s into a rarely opened drawer.

Another friend drinks white Russians to "sneak up on his liver – it thinks it's milk."

I was putting gas in my car the other day and started thinking about the little tricks we play on ourselves and others to save time or money simply for the tiny thrill of getting away with something.

Am I the only one who tries to get that last drop of fuel from the nozzle before the price jumps to the next cent? You give the handle a quick squeeze and watch the display on the pump. Sometimes you win, other times you have to dig a penny out of your ashtray.

And how many people set their alarm clock a few minutes fast? Mine is 15 minutes fast, but since I know it's 15 minutes fast, I've defeated the purpose and still oversleep.

The idea that should work, but never does, is the concept of using the "last channel" button on the remote to watch two shows at once. We should be able to press the button during a commercial on one channel and catch a full three minutes of the other show, but it never works this way. There's always a commercial on the other channel at the same time. The networks need to do something about this.

And what about the shampoo phenomenon of filling up a near-empty bottle with water? I know I'm not the only one who does this. Except I don't do it to get the most for my money or for any economically practical reason.

For me, it's because I have not planned ahead by grabbing a new bottle out of the linen closet before getting into the shower. The unopened bottle remains in the closet a good three feet away from the shower, and I hate getting out and then back in. I end up either soaking the floor and subsequently slipping, or I wrap a towel around me thereby canceling out the comfort of a dry towel after the shower.

The shampoo strategy is a little like my practice of moving light-bulbs rather than buying new ones. Don't get me wrong, I'm certainly not opposed to spending $1.29 on new bulbs, it's just that I never think about buying them until the bulb in my desk lamp has replaced the one on my nightstand, which moved to the bathroom when that one burned out.

And have you ever tried to speed up the cooking process by increasing the oven temperature? It doesn't work, I promise. Ask the pizza delivery guy who wound up at my front door squinting through the smoke.

That's a little game we only play once, unlike the strategy of returning someone's phone call when you know they won't be home. We've all done it. You fulfill the obligation of returning the call without having to carry through with a lengthy, and often unpleasant conversation.

Of course, the same people could easily be playing the same game with you so your relationship is eventually reduced to a series of phone messages left on your home phone in the middle of a workday. Sometimes it's best that way.

Another illogical little strategy I find myself using is the theory that I'll have a better chance of making it to the gas station if I drive faster on fumes. I know, I use more gas by going faster, and therefore have no better chance of making it there, but it seems like a good idea when I'm just a few blocks from the Chevron.

It also seems like a good idea to keep bills in the mailbox until I have sufficient funds to write the checks. The "out of sight, out of mind" philosophy has always worked for me, and once I bring the electric bill inside the house, it sits on the counter staring, and making me feel guilty for putting the air-conditioner on high.

Of course, I wouldn't need to use this trick if I could learn to hide money from myself.

June 9, 2002

Think about it:
Jellyfish are 95% water.

IN THE NEIGHBORHOOD

I can't decide whether I'm naïve or stupid. (And I'm not asking your opinion.)

I tried to be a good neighbor. I gave someone the benefit of the doubt. I did what I would like to think someone else would do for me.

I got screwed.

Worse, I became jaded and distrustful.

A man knocked on my door last Friday night while I was battling for possession of the remote control. I retreated temporarily from the clicker war to speak with the smallish, dark-haired man. I had never seen him before, but he introduced himself and said he and his partner own the antique store two doors down.

His fidgety demeanor seemed to mesh with his tale of being locked out of the shop and apartment and needing to take a cab to Key Haven to retrieve cash and keys.

I initially assumed he needed to use the phone to call a cab. Well, he did need that, but he also needed cab fare, which he promised to repay in an hour and a half.

All right, all right, half of you are now rolling your eyes and asking how stupid I could be. We're all familiar with Key West, and we've seen what substance abuse looks like in a person with sunken eyes, a lower jaw that's in constant motion and eyes that just can't focus.

The rest of you are still reading to find out how long it took the guy to come back and repay his debt.

Stop wondering. He never came back. Not that night, not the next day, not in a week. And I learned from a neighbor that his first introduction to the so-called antique dealer named Alan had been identical as was the encounter a woman down the street had with him.

Surprise, surprise, it seems Alan has a bit of a crack habit.

And the actual owner of the antique shop in question (I stopped in on Sunday) insisted he does not have any business partners, although he does know Alan who apparently has no phone. The shop owner agreed to let Alan know that I had been in looking for him the next time he saw him, and then accepted my business card as a way to get in touch with me.

Nothing.

By then my anger with myself had been replaced by anger with Alan. I tried the whole liberal, sympathetic approach in which I pitied Alan and cursed the society that led to his addiction and desperation. That didn't last long.

This dirtbag had taken money from me, money I worked hard for, money I lent him in kindness – money I don't spend on crack.

Sure it was only $30, but tell that to BellSouth, which is consequently waiting until next pay day to receive their $30 from me. I'm not the only one in this town who lives from one paycheck to the next with every bill paid carefully so as to ensure that money will actually be in the account when the company tries to deposit the check. Like many others, I have paid bills a few days late while waiting for my next paycheck, but only the ones that don't charge a late fee.

Thirty dollars is not a lot of money, but it's everything in the final days before payday. It's lunch, gas, pasta for dinner, a few Diet Cokes and maybe a glass of wine, maybe. But it's not for crack, and I've never knocked on a stranger's door at 10:30 at night to borrow money for a Diet Coke – or cab fare.

Alan took something that was mine and lied to me. I don't know what I would have done if he had introduced himself as the crackhead next door who needed $30 for a buzz. But that didn't happen, so we'll never know.

I realize I'm not the only person to have been taken advantage of. I know there are others who are even more trusting than I and who have lost more than $30 in these transactions. I also realize I have a tremendous advantage in that I have a public forum in which to vent my anger, frustration and disappointment in my neighbor.

So I figure this column is for everyone else who has ever tried to do the right thing and had it blow up in their face – or wallet. I hope we'll continue to find goodness in others – unless they're fidgeting on my front porch on a Friday night. Oh, I also hope I see Alan again real soon. He has something that belongs to me.

April 27, 2003

RULES OF YOUTH

Remember when you weren't allowed to cross the street by yourself, ghost runners made kickball possible and everyone in the neighborhood had to be in when the street lights came on.

Whether you grew up in the Midwest, Northeast or Deep South, the rules of childhood remain basically unchallenged and are as universal as the metallic taste that comes from drinking water out of a garden hose.

Sure, there are some variations as to how much money goes into Free Parking on the Monopoly board. Only some kickball games allow "pegging," a semi-barbaric variation that involves hurling the rubber ball at the base runner, and only the luckiest kids are allowed to sleep at a friend's house on a school night.

But for the most part, the guidelines are as steadfast as grass stains.

Too bad the rules aren't as concise in the grown-up world. Kids don't have time for exceptions, emotions and logic. As a kid, if you don't like the rules, you can take your ball and go home – unless, of course, yours is the only ball available in which case you get to make the rules.

Kid rules could be beneficial in the adult world. Then again, so could Big Wheels and Sit'n'Spins.

Think of how useful the phrase, "Doesn't count, do over" would be in work and relationship situations.

Write a bad check for a cell phone bill?

"Doesn't count, Sprint, do over."

Berate your boss in an accidentally audible tones?

"Doesn't count, my gifted employer, do over."

And what if there existed a light pole, front porch or mailbox somewhere in town that was dubbed "base."

As long as your hand or foot is somehow touching it, whoever is "it" can't get you – nothing bad can happen on base.

Of course, in keeping with the rules, you can't spend the whole day there, but are welcome to stop and catch your breath before re-entering the "game."

While I, personally, have had a difficult time convincing bosses and boyfriends that "rock, paper, scissors" is the best way to settle disputes, think how much simpler life would be if the other person immediately gave in upon hearing, "I'm gonna tell."

Meetings, appointments, happy hour and vacations would be much easier to plan if your friends all gathered at a designated spot when someone called "ollie, ollie oxen free."

What if the ice cream man's tune at the end of the block was enough to abbreviate board meetings, and minor discrepancies could be settled by asking a supposedly unbiased adult to think of a number between 1 and 15? The one who picks the closer number without going over wins whatever was in dispute.

And that rule about kids being relegated to the front porch while wielding dripping Popsicles? Good idea, Mom.

Unfortunately, there is now a decidedly lime stain on my couch. (And yes, I might be the only person in the world who likes lime Popsicles.)

The lime stain is actually all right because it matches the small green spot on my white linen shirt – obviously I had not changed from "good clothes" to "play clothes" before eating the Popsicle. Another good one, Mom.

There was also something to be said for being grounded.

Of course, at the time, the weekend you spent indoors rather than outside seemed to last an eternity and no one was meaner than your parents.

But in adult life, police officers can be somewhat more intimidating than parents, especially if you've broken a big rule. I think the cops should be able to "ground" people.

There's not always a need to go through the tedium of paperwork, handcuffs and bond money. What if the officers could just send you home with orders to remain indoors for the next three days. Hell, they could even have the power to unplug the phone and take away our television privileges.

I actually wish someone, anyone had grounded me last weekend – I certainly wasn't home by the time the streetlights came on.

July 19, 2002

WAITING FOR WEDNESDAY

photo: roboneal.com

Santa Claus was drinking in Turtle Kraals this week. I swear. Apparently he had all of his Christmas chores finished and was just waiting for Wednesday. You gotta love Christmas in the Keys. Santa's drinking bourbon, Mrs. Claus is drinking rum and everyone else is drinking anything they can find at the hundreds of holiday parties that have crippled many employees. It's not a bad time of year, really. Until you look at your bank balance or your waistline.

But there are a few minor Yuletide aggravations I think we could all do without:

• Running out of tape in the middle of wrapping a gift. You've already covered the box in paper and were able to get one end of the box neatly folded down and taped securely. But while holding the paper together at the other end, you hear that annoying squeak that symbolizes the end of the Scotch tape roll. Have you ever resorted to stamps, or the sticky stripe at the top of Post-it notes, or even Band Aids? You know you can roll them up into an adhesive cylinder and stick them on the inside of the paper so they don?t show. Trust me, I never buy enough tape.

• Burning the bottom of sugar cookies. Why do they have to be so delicate? I mean, really. They're only cookies for crying out loud, they should be able to stand a little heat. And how come the bottoms can be totally blackened when the tops are barely that perfect golden blonde color?

• Getting a pine needle stuck between your toes when walking through the living room. Apparently, the vacuum cleaner has a sick, sick mind of its own and just enjoys leaving a few needles behind.

• Running out of wrapping paper so that there's a stripe of box showing. I know, it's a minor aggravation and a bit of a pet peeve of mine. I spent four summers in the gift-wrapping department of a candy store and have a bit of a compulsion when it comes to making gifts look nice.

• Hearing the opening notes of "O Come All Ye Faithful," but then realizing that it's actually the "Adeste Fidelis." I graduated from a Catholic high school, and have sung my share of holiday hymns, but still can never figure out the Latin words until they get to the "adoramus" part at the end that always builds into a cool crescendo.

• Forgetting which wrapped box contains what. In other words,

Gram's handkerchiefs and stationery are in the same size box as the X-rated gag gift of pasta shaped like body parts that you got for...well, never mind.

• Having to continually add names to your shopping list. Ever run into someone whom you had absolutely no intention of buying a gift for? Then they say, "Hey, great to see you, I just found the perfect Christmas gift for you, I can't wait for you to open it." You smile warmly and say you're thrilled. Then you add something about having a gift for them, but it's at home and is not yet wrapped. These people might not know it, but are often victims of "regifting." That is, you give them something you've already gotten from someone else.

• Always being in the wrong shopping center for whichever store you're aiming for. This one is specific to Key West, and even more specifically to North Roosevelt Boulevard. While wandering through Kmart and getting frustrated by the self checkout aisles that were all out of order, I thought of the perfect gift for someone at Pier 1. So I was on my way to the other shopping center and was turning left into the Winn-Dixie parking lot when I realized I still had to get my brother gift at Blockbuster.

This sort of madness went on for about two more round trips between Searstown and the Overseas Market all while being subjected to "Grandma got run over by a reindeer" on at least two radio stations.

But with that nightmare complete, I was able to head home with most of my shopping complete. Sure, I was broke and exhausted and still fuming about the Kmart disaster, but the guest houses on Truman Avenue lit up the night sky. The American flag on the bike shop was illuminated by moonlight and I was on my way to see Santa at Turtle Kraals.

Merry Christmas, Key West!
December 22, 2002

THE EARLY BIRD - GETS TIRED

I'm not a morning person.

I can usually answer the phone in a voice convincing enough to assure pre-noon callers I've been up for hours, but that's about the extent of it.

Don't get me wrong, I've tried the whole morning thing – not always voluntarily – but I've seen how the sunlight is different, more delicate, at that time of day. I've noticed the temperature and the way the heat and humidity seem to sleep in allowing the breeze to inhabit the morning.

I've gotten up early on a Saturday, washed my car and read a few newspapers all before breakfast.

I can appreciate Saturday morning productivity, but not as much as I appreciate those precious two hours of slumber that barely bridge the gap between dream and reality. You're alert enough to know the world's awake outside your window, but still asleep enough to have those dreams that start out somewhat normally, but end with a midget chasing your third-grade teacher through your office. But it wasn't really your office, but in the dream it was your office. Or the ones so realistic you later find yourself asking your best friend about a conversation you may or may not have had. I love those dreams more than I love early mornings.

I also love late afternoons after the beach – when my hair's still crispy with the salt and sun. I can't run my fingers through it, but it looks inexplicably all right when thrown carelessly back with a cheap clip.

Growing up at the beach, I've always loved that time of day when the world (at least, my world) teeters between afternoon and evening, lunch and dinner, as if the sun, still hovering, has momentarily forgotten its responsibilities. It's porch time, and it lends itself to chip-and-dip snacks guaranteed to ruin my dinner. And for some reason, a Diet Coke, poured into one of those fish-filled acrylic glasses always tastes better right after the beach.

The sunburn that'll evolve painfully after the shower and throughout the night has not yet appeared and I don't have anything to do.

My options are endless. I can pore over a few more chapters of the book I was reading on the beach. I can take another stab at the crossword puzzle I gave up on at the beach or I can sit idly on the balcony staring down at people and playing my own little game of guessing which ones will look up. The game gets even better when I actually know the person looking up, although the ensuing conversation from sidewalk to balcony tends to interrupt such a game.

I admit, the air's a little warmer and slightly uncomfortable in the afternoon. The breeze ran away with the morning joggers and chickens are the only birds chirping.

But this is Key West, the island of snooze buttons and naps. Not much happens before 10:30 a.m. on weekdays, noon on weekends and 2 p.m. after Fantasy Fest and on New Year's Day.

Besides, the people who rave about the fragility of the sunrise over Houseboat Row are usually tired by 9 p.m., and plenty happens after 9 p.m.

Million-dollar deals evolve from cocktail napkins and merlot. Happy hour becomes a late dinner. Coworkers stop talking about work and friends start talking about the weekend. Employees dance with bosses. Chicken wings gain popularity, and political opinions are shared. Rented movies flicker across television screens. Shoes are abandoned under coffee tables, and pizzas are delivered. Kids have bad dreams and parents watch R-rated movies.

The afternoons, evenings and nights offer plenty – without the chipper morning joggers. Who's got time for mornings? I'm still trying to figure out why my third-grade teacher was in my office with a midget.

February 10, 2002

Think about it:
The American Corporate Hall of Fame in Toledo, Ohio exhibits cocktail napkins, matchbooks and bar bills on which great corporations were conceived.

DIETARY SUPPLEMENT

Does anyone actually prefer the taste of carrot sticks to Doritos?

And, if, in some bizarre alternate universe, Doritos were found to be a health food and carrots were deemed "junk food," would we then crave a handful of carrot sticks as a midnight snack?

I don't think so – not if they still tasted like carrots.

But seriously, do those fitness-craved, aggravatingly chipper people who eat carrots as a snack actually enjoy them as much as the rest of the world savors that spoonful of ice cream secreted out of the freezer before dinner? Do they like Dannon fat-free yogurt better than that delectable mound of peanut butter we lick off a knife even though we have no intention of making a sandwich, and actually sometimes skip the knife and use our index finger?

I wish I was the sort of person who had strong cravings for a huge garden salad with fat-free dressing. It doesn't happen. If it did, wouldn't Dominos be slammed on Friday nights hurriedly delivering salads?

My diets tend to ebb and flow based on several factors – the contents of my fridge, the pizza coupons affixed to the fridge with a magnetic chip clip, the degree of physical exertion I put forth within the previous 24 to 36 hours and number of pairs of jeans I can't fit into.

Many people swear that after a good, long workout, they really are inspired to eat a light, healthy meal so as not to negate the workout. Sure, it makes sense, I get it.

But for me, that healthy post-exercise salad just becomes an appetizer for the main course – pizza bagels and ice cream.

I also have an uncanny ability to convince myself that I did much more exercise than I actually did.

By the time the cheese is melted on the second pizza bagel, my 45-minute power walk has evolved into a 10K run – hell, it was an all-out sprint – no wonder I'm so hungry.

These conversations with myself usually lead to one of those covert dips into the jar of Jif as I wait for the toaster oven to make that cheese crispy and golden brown.

Now, I do have (a little) willpower and there are times I eat nothing but Popsicles and bananas for two or three days. Of course, that's usually the days before payday when there's about $6 in my checking account and three of them have to be used for gas so I can actually get to work and thereby increase my chances of receiving a paycheck.

What did we do before the magic of debit cards, when you could only take money from an ATM in multiples of 20?

I can't believe I wasn't emaciated on the side of the road and out of gas more often.

But back to the whimsy of my diets. I not only reward myself for exercise with food, I reward myself for eating healthy – with more food. Seriously.

Conversely, I also tend to drown my sorrows and cure my hangovers with anything other than vegetables. An exhausting and frustrating day at work? Nothing a half a bag of Tostitos and some processed, spicy cheese dip won't fix.

A late Friday night that turned into an early Saturday morning, leaving me weakened and nauseated? No worries, that's what Pringles and pizza were made for.

I keep telling myself that one of these days I will get serious about a diet for more than three days. I tell myself that a cheesesteak with fried onions is an acceptable dinner given I had eaten only a salad for lunch. (I just as easily forget about the brownie that followed the salad, and the Snickers that was calling my name from the officer vending machine.) I tell myself that my fitness regime would be amazingly enhanced by a healthy diet instead of power walks and fries. Unfortunately, I tell myself these things seconds before the toaster signals the crisp perfection of a golden pizza bagel.

March 30, 2003

Think about it:
You consume 1/2 a calorie everytime
you lick a stamp.

The woman in the produce department had gotten a speeding ticket in Big Pine, and the guy buying lightbulbs had just bought a new scooter from a friend who moved away.

I didn't converse with these people, but I now know tidbits about the lives of complete strangers.

Cell phones are here to stay. The communication devices that get smaller by the month have become an inextricable part of our lives.

Oh sure, there exists a rather self-righteous few who smile smugly, boasting about how they've managed to evade the electronic leash and remain free from new voicemails and interrupting rings.

But have you noticed they're also the ones asking to borrow other people's phones in the event of a missed plane, change of plans, wrong turn or emergency?

They're the ones who roll their eyes at people with phones as if to say, "Just how important do you think you are?"

But when something goes awry, they get a baleful look in their eyes.

"I forgot to call my boss and let him know the meeting was changed," they say, panicking, their eyes darting slyly to the phone on the counter or strapped to a belt. "Could I borrow your phone – I promise I'll only be a second. Will it cost you money? I'll give you a couple bucks."

Without fail, the phone is handed over and the panicked party usually stares at it, puzzled, for a split second pretending they're unfamiliar with the technology that forces them to press "send" or "talk" before the ringing begins.

Yeah right, like they haven't borrowed hundreds of other phones from hundreds of other people.

I have a cell phone, and I love it. But I understand the complaints rendered about them and admit they can be distracting, intrusive and frustrating.

People talk too loud. They no longer remember phone numbers. The digits are saved in internal phonebooks – handy until rendered useless by an expected plunge into a pool.

The electronic version of Fur Elise has interrupted otherwise pleasant lunches, and I'm guilty of trying to turn left onto North Roosevelt Boulevard while checking messages and digging a piping hot French fry out of the McDonald's bag. (Disclaimer: Talking on a cell phone while driving can be dangerous, distracting and is illegal in some states.)

The cell phone debate is a staticky one, but the world could be a little less intrusive if a universal etiquette were established.

First, they should be set to vibrate during meals and meetings, and should never be answered at the table.

Second, there's no reason to scream into the little piece of technology. If you're not being heard by the person on the other end of the line, but the baby down the block just woke up, hang up and try your call later.

Third, do not "shush" others, or throw glaring looks at people going about their daily lives while you're on the phone in a public place.

Just because you're on the phone doesn't mean the scooter cannot honk its horn or the toddler cannot shriek.

If you need complete silence for your call, do not go outside with the phone and expect the world to whisper.

Fourth, if you'd rather the entire island not know about the rash that's clearing up nicely, don't talk about it in the salad dressing aisle of the grocery store.

And lastly, every once in a while, hang up and talk to people, in person, face to face. They smile, they laugh, and they put their arms around you, even if they can't remember your phone number.

October 21, 2001

Think about it:
Cell phones' biggest enemy in Key West?
Saltwater.

GET REAL

When is it going to end? When will "real people" stop invading my television? I have officially had my fill of reality television. I, like you, live my own life and it's pretty realistic.

I work. I play. My friends aggravate me, and make me who I am. I get frustrated at work, and have moments of triumph there. I oversleep. I get phone calls from people I haven't heard from in years and ignore phone calls (thanks to the miracle of caller ID) from people I don't necessarily want to speak with.

I laugh at old "Cheers" re-runs and still cry when Goose dies in "Top Gun," and I know I'm not alone.

We all live our own lives however different they may be. I treat myself to a steak dinner when they're on sale at Albertson's and I eat Campbell's soup that requires the addition of water rather than milk when my fridge is empty.

I don't do all these things on a deserted island. I don't have to build my own shelter every night, and disagreements with friends don't result in me losing a million dollars. I'm not tested to see how I get along on a blind date. I don't have to eat live bugs, and so far, five gay guys haven't barged in and remodeled my apartment.

It surprises me that Americans have put up with this programming for so long now. It's been, what, four years now since "Survivor" introduced us to life on that island and the threat of being voted off? And I was hooked. I watched the winner the first season get naked on the beach and win a bunch of money. The same season, I also watched couples test the boundaries of their relationships on "Temptation Island." If you didn't watch it (and it's probably best if you don't admit to it) the scenery in Belize was beautiful and the relationship aspect was like craning your neck to see a car accident.

I've watched my share, but it's gone far enough. (Truth be told, I watched two seasons of "Survivor" and was lured into "Temptation Island" by someone else whose otherwise rational demeanor gave way to a fun obsession with soap-opera drama on prime time television.)

People are now trying to marry off their fathers on prime time television, and others are choosing between a guy they really like and a million dollars.

I may have gotten the specifics of the love or money show wrong and will get a flood of e-mails correcting me. It will just prove how many of us are into it, how willing we are to concern ourselves with other people's dramas.

Look at "American Idol." I never watched a single episode, but television executives have been shoving the winners at us since the has-been or never-will-be judges chose their favorite – with the help of middle America.

We, as the American public, haven't always made the best choices. We liked parachute pants at one point. Enough of us bought Tab soda to keep it in cans for far too long. Are you going to trust the society that brought you "Three's Company" to give you an idol?

Why should we care which stranger loves another stranger, which stranger can't get along with other strangers living in the same house?

Why do we end up caring about which guy another guy chooses to share a vacation with, or which woman has the will to chew and swallow live worms?

The sensationalism and absurdity of other people's lives fascinate us. But we live in reality, well, most of us do. I'll never get a million dollars for getting along with my friends or family and I don't think I'll ever have to choose between them and money. I'll never have to eat fish slime to prove my worth, or vote someone off our fair island, as enticing as the idea is. I've seen enough. I'll pay attention to my own life, and no one has to film it – unless someone thinks it's worth a million bucks.

September 14, 2003

SMALL(ER) WORLD

Say what you will, but air travel has made the world smaller, more accessible. Whether you fear it, distrust it or are frequently frustrated by it, it provides more opportunities than ever before.

And it forces us to interact with people we would otherwise never encounter in our daily lives – and that's not always a good thing. It becomes easy to despise people who share check-in lines and overhead compartments with us.

The relationship among passengers begins in the check-in line at about the same time we're all scanning the crowd to determine whether the flight will be full, or if there's a chance we won't have to sit directly next to any of those people.

Thus the animosity begins. Immediately, every other passenger is a threat to the potentially empty seat next to you. Have you ever shared that exalted moment with the person in the same row when you both realize that the plane's doors have closed and no one is getting into the seat between? You exchange knowing smiles and settle back, deciding individually whether to leave the armrest on your side down, or swing it up for more room. In that instant, you and the passenger two seats away have become allies. You might never utter a word, but you're in this thing together and have shared a small victory.

On the other hand, it's equally easy to hold a personal grudge against the poor schmuck who sits in that middle seat just as you and the other guy are starting, albeit prematurely, to get your hopes up.

It's also easy to dislike people who wait in the check-in line for 25 minutes, but for some reason act surprised when the ticket agent asks to see their ID. So, of course, they have to dig through the mountains of luggage (as if they don't always keep their wallet in the same place.)

And then there's the people who, for some reason, never grasp the concept of boarding from the rear of the plane, and therefore insist on standing directly in front of the gate holding a boarding pass that says Seat 7C. And they usually insist they have some special reason to "pre-board." Last time I listened to the boarding announcements, the agents didn't include ignorance and impatience as acceptable reasons to get on the plane before everyone else.

It really is easy to develop an intense and internalized repulsion for some of these people, especially when traveling alone, minding your own business, following all the rules and choosing not to scream at an airline employee when a flight is delayed. Because, really, it's their fault the jet didn't leave Detroit on time – in the middle of that storm. And that ticket agent really is the person who can make the plane fly faster so as not to disrupt anyone's schedule.

Let's not forget the obnoxious passengers who get on the plane drunk and proceed to get even more so – all while thinking they're entertaining others with jokes about the air sickness bag and their willingness to help with the emergency exit.

And then there's those exceedingly pleasant fellow travelers who do nothing but complain – about their seats, the delay, the temperature inside the plane, inside the airport and outside at their destination and the shortage of pillows for the flight.

The abundance of unacceptable people in airports is staggering. But it makes you appreciate even more those few who make your trip bearable. Maybe it's a well-behaved child who shares his animal crackers, or a businessman with whom you share your newspaper, who then hands over his small package of pretzels in gratitude.

These little exchanges show the human side of, well, humans and are to be appreciated. Because while air travel has made the world smaller, planes are rarely big enough for the personalities of everyone who stood in that check-in line.

September 28, 2003

Think about it:
Aviation history for the Florida Keys began in 1913 when Augustin Parla flew a bi-wing seaplane from Key West to Cuba.

WHAT'S IN A NAME?

photo: roboneal.com

Anyone been to the old Brooklyn Boyz lately? How about the new Camille's – where the Full Moon Saloon stood several years ago?

Some buildings, areas and businesses in town have undergone renovations, foreclosures, police raids and every other change in usage and signage, yet will always retain the moniker that yielded the most notoriety, infamy or longevity.

The "old Brooklyn Boyz" has been about six different things in the past three and a half years, yet few have bothered to learn the new names, and even fewer could name the succession of replacements.

The property that now houses Camille's on Simonton Street will forever be remembered by many as the Full Moon Saloon, although most will readily admit that they don't remember much of what they did inside the once-popular watering hole.

Remember Winky's on Flagler? Has anyone bothered to notice, or remember that it's now the Palm Tree and has been for more than four years? They're still open all night, and we all still stop in for drinks, cigarettes, milk and lottery tickets. But the sign has definitely changed.

The collective, or should I say selective, memory of this town never ceases to astound me. We forgive major infractions and forget former roommates as soon as the last electric bill is paid, but always remember the name of an obscure bar that closed a decade ago and has since been a hair salon, T-shirt shop, sandwich joint and empty storefront.

And the town's legendary characters, including politicians and officials, have long been forgiven for any past indiscretions, bribery, sex scandals and DUIs. Their shortcomings are a thing of the past by the time the next piece of scandal erupts.

We don't remember the theme from last year's Fantasy Fest or the name of the hurricane that threatened the island last fall, but half the town still refers to the building near the south end of Duval Street as Viva Zapata.

It cracks me up that Jerky's on Caroline Street is Red's to some, and Longshots to others, depending on how long you've lived here.

The nicely decorated signs might call the bight the Historic Seaport, but many residents will never call it that.

And has anyone started calling the Duval Beach Club by its real name? No, we're saying "the old South Beach restaurant," or "the new Kelly's."

The brand new conglomeration of shops and offices at the bottom of Simonton Street is now, officially, Simonton Row. Yeah right, it'll always be the Strunk building.

The former Oak Beach Inn has yet another name now, but will be the Hooters property for awhile, I'm sure. Well, Shorty's hasn't been a diner for more than 10 years, the old El Cacique has been a bike shop for years, but some still refer to it as "that old Cuban place," or the place across the street from the Hog's Breath, which was, of course, the Monster.

Businesses change names, locations and owners at an alarming rate, but residents are slower to adjust. Are we clinging to memories of the way things used to be, or just not concerned enough to learn the new name?

I remember the first time an old Conch referred to the Fausto's on White Street as Gulfstream. Now how long has that been?

Will newcomers who arrive in five years ever understand why we call a certain area on South Roosevelt Boulevard Houseboat Row? And will T.J.'s Fudgecycle ever lose its distinction as being the old Boca Chica Bar? Will anyone remember where Diva's was, or stop calling the little shop across from Mangoes Smok'n Edna's?

How long will it take us to start writing Keys Energy Services on our checks instead of City Electric Service, and what will Brooklyn Boyz be called next?

May 26, 2002

AH, SUMMER

I admit its arrival no longer heralds the intrigue and excitement it once did, but it's summertime and remember how it used to be?

Oh all right, it's not exactly summer, but it's Memorial Day weekend, and where I grew up that was close enough.

I know a lot of us did not grow up in Key West, and our summers were marked by more than a calendar page and the ability to wake up late.

In a town where it's warm all year, summer sort of gets lost in the shuffle. It's just warmer, and there's no longer that huge traffic snarl on Flagler Avenue every afternoon in the school zones. Then again, I'm an adult now, so all summer means is increased power bills and more severe sunburns.

But I spent most of my youth in the Northeast, the Jersey Shore to be exact, and summer was a state of mind that simmered just below the surface all spring and nearly boiled over on the first hot day we were allowed to wear shorts to school. Summer didn't just signal the end of school, it marked the beginning of three months of unparalleled delight in doing nothing, or doing whatever you wanted – until curfew.

Wednesday is the last day of school for kids in the Keys, and I'm jealous. Summer meant so much. And remember how it changed as we got older?

As a little, tiny kid, I lived in the Midwest – Kansas and Nebraska – and summer meant grass stains on my knees rather than my jeans, drinks slurped from a garden hose rather than a glass and bikes hastily discarded on front lawns as we headed to the backyard to run through the sprinkler.

In the Midwest, it was a time for daily trips to the community pool, where I learned to swim, jump off the diving board and devour frozen Snickers bars.

Was there anything more frustrating than the "adult swim" at the local pool, or am I the only one who had to suffer through this monstrosity? Our pool in Kansas City, Blue Jacket, had decided some adults did not find it altogether amusing to be constantly splashed, landed on and jumped over while trying to cool off, so every hour the lifeguards made the kids get out of the pool for 10 minutes so the adults could simply stand there in the water.

Seriously, they just stood there. Where's the fun in that? They didn't dive for tossed pennies or scream "Marco Polo" over and over. Some of them didn't even get their hair wet, but instead scooped water over their upper arms and face. Some of the cooler dads, mine included, would throw a Nerf ball back and forth with one of the other cooler dads, but adult swim was pretty much the bane of our existence – and imaging the chaotic line that formed at the snack bar when the kids couldn't be in the water. It took forever to get a frozen Snickers or a lime "freeze pop."

Ah, summer.

And it all changed as we got older.

I moved to the Jersey Shore, which meant summers looked like any postcard you've ever seen from that area – long stretches of beach with pounding waves and lifeguard stands at each block, and more than two miles of boardwalk, home to unlimited pizza, French fries, arcade games and surf shops. And salt water taffy, let us never forget salt water taffy.

I'll never be able to forget that stuff after spending four summers sorting through it and gift wrapping boxes of it for my first summer job on the Ocean City boardwalk.

Summer also meant summer love. We've all had our share of suntanned heartthrobs, who, in looking back, seemed to disappear around Labor Day just as we were shopping for school clothes.

Maybe they worked at a favorite pizza place, or twirled their lifeguard whistles on the beach while smiling from behind Ray Bans. Maybe they operated the roller coaster at the boardwalk amusement rides, and then showed up on your porch nervously shaking your father's hand promising to have you back by midnight.

Ah, summer. Regardless of the year round temperature, or my status as an adult, it's here and it's a perfect excuse for a frozen Snickers.

May 25, 2003

IN YOUR EYES

"My junior prom date is engaged."

That's how my friend Kate started her e-mail the other day. She was sitting in her office at the San Diego Opera Company (seriously, it's a real place) apparently thinking of Adam Smith – the guy who puked in his hat at the homecoming dance. The one who had signed up for cross-country just to get a varsity letter and ended up hiding under the bleachers at our field hockey practice until the daily run was over.

He's getting married in Miami sometime next year – to someone other than Kate, who never actually dated him as far as I can recall.

But her message made me think of my junior prom date, who is, in fact, married to a girl named Mandy.

Suddenly, the opera music that normally runs through my mind when reading a message from Kate was replaced by Peter Gabriel's "In Your Eyes."

"The light, the heat, in your eyes, I am complete, in your eyes...."

The glint of metallic confetti once again bounced off the hardwood floor of the high school gym. Kate was dancing with Adam and I was swaying back and forth with Drew in the midst of another 100 or so pendulum-like couples. A flask of something passed among us in the darkened gym and a slimy-looking guy in an iridescent suit was taking pictures in the gym lobby. His white trellis with its fake pillars and flowers was set up in front of the trophy case. And although the bathroom was filled with people in formal wear, it was still part of a locker room that was still the color of Gulden's mustard.

But that night, everything was perfect, including the comfortable ease of my jeans and sweater later that night at the "after-party." A bunch of kids sat around someone's basement drinking beers we thought no one would miss. The guys played pool and kept changing the music while the girls made mean comments about the dress – or date – of another girl, who was at a different "afterparty" saying similar things about us.

It was high school. It was the slamming of metal lockers every 43 minutes and essay questions about "Hamlet." It was the prom king walking his girlfriend to her car, leaning into her window, squinting

113

against the sun and kissing her good-bye. It was substitute teachers on the day of a test and early dismissals. It was cutting first period to have breakfast at the diner and blaming the tardiness on traffic. It was state championship basketball games and garage bands. It meant yearbook pictures and parties when parents were out of town.

High school also meant driver's licenses, which, in my family, didn't mean immediate permission to drive.

"Just because the state of New Jersey says you can drive, doesn't mean I do," was my father's mantra for my last year of high school.

Someone here in the Keys must be taking his driver's test next week, and someone else's parents are going away for a week in September.

Yep, kids have headed back to school and by now the newness has worn off. They've flipped through the textbooks to see who used it last year. The material at the end of the book looks daunting and teachers have started handing out assignments in earnest.

But the unmistakable energy of the marching band on a football field soon will fill the air. Last year's homecoming queen will hand over her crown, and report cards will be sent home. A few Saturday mornings will be taken up by the SAT. Some teens will will fall in love and cafeteria food will be judged harshly.

Come spring, the song will be different and the gym will be different, but a hundred couples will cling to each other during slow songs and pass a flask back and forth. (Disclaimer: I am not condoning underage drinking, but I do choose to live in reality.)

They'll have no idea that the night will prompt an e-mail message 10 years from now, when the guy who puked in his hat sophomore year gets engaged and the girl who danced with him works for an opera company.

But that's all right, they're not supposed to think about that. It's high school and there's metallic confetti on the gym floor. That's all that matters.

August 17, 2003

THANKS A LITTLE

Is there a turkey made of traced handprints on your fridge? Are there a few pints of heavy whipping cream inside your fridge? Are you having to recall the details of trigonometry to determine how to seat and feed eight people in an apartment that doesn't have a dining room or its accompanying table?

That's all right, just loosen up the drawstring on those pants and pop open a bottle of this year's Beaujolais. I know I'm thankful for drawstring pants and seasonal red wine. I'm thankful for all the major things we're supposed to be thankful for, too.

But sometimes it's not the major things in life that give us pause on the last Thursday of November, but the little miracles that happen every day.

They're not earth-shattering or life-affirming, but they do permit us a brief sigh of relief or moment of thanks and allow us to continue on with our day and our lives.

For example, I'm thankful every time the toilet – any toilet – looks as if it might overflow when the water keeps climbing quietly toward the rim, but then miraculously begins to recede. You watch it with wide eyes willing it to go down, perhaps adding some pantomime hand gestures to "push" the water back into the toilet. And then once it does ebb away from the rim, you stand there watching for a few more seconds, exhale sharply and make your escape.

I'm just a little bit grateful every time the folks at the Taco Bell drive-thru remember that I asked them nicely to skip the sour cream on my nacho supreme. It's not a dietary restriction or anything, I'm eating at Taco Bell, aren't I? I just hate sour cream. And I rarely get to give thanks for this little victory because it almost never happens.

Another exhilarating moment of relief and thanksgiving comes the morning after a middle-of-the-night power outage. You open your eyes realizing it's light out, but you haven't heard your alarm, which is blinking on the nightstand.

There's a few instants while you're looking for your watch or switching on the television to find out what time it is when you're not sure whether it's still rather early or if it's nearing noon, you're impossibly late for one thing and have completely missed something else. When you finally learn your alarm wouldn't have gone off for another 90 minutes, life is good.

And how about the murmured "Oh, thank god" we let out when we find our wallet wedged between a friend's couch cushions the day after we discovered it missing but the day before we set about canceling credit cards and getting a new license. That's a good feeling even when the wallet's empty of any cash.

Cash elicits that small sentiment of thanks when it's found wadded up but crispy in the pocket of a clean pair of jeans. I like the way cash stays together after a spin cycle, but that business card I shoved in my back pocket becomes lint.

I'm thankful every time my windshield remains blissfully free of parking tickets despite the questionable nature of the parking spot I selected.

Sometimes, but not often, I'm thankful for a wet and cloudy Saturday so I can lounge on the couch watching movies starring Judith Light without feeling like I should be at the beach or doing something outside where the rest of the upright people are.

And what about that little moment of relief that comes after a soda tips over on the floor of the car, and upon picking it up you realize only a few drops escaped through the straw hole in the plastic lid? That soda often tips while I'm in the middle of making a wild, lurching left turn onto a two-way thoroughfare, so I'm also thankful when the traffic parts just briefly allowing me to make my turn.

I'm thankful that as an adult I no longer have to make those handprint turkeys out of brown construction paper. Mine never looked right. Ever.

Besides, the only time I saw a turkey in my house at Thanksgiving each year, it looked nothing like the strutting, feathered friend schoolchildren always called "Tom."

November 23, 2003

WE'LL SURVIVE

Hang in there, we'll survive. We always do.

But it's hot. We have officially reached that time of year when the temperature becomes a jumping-off point in many conversations around town.

"Man, it's hot out there."

"Come over here, let's stand in the shade."

"Where do you feel like going tonight?"

"Someplace with air-conditioning."

Sound familiar?

It is the middle of August, which means it's only the middle of summer in the Florida Keys.

Unlike our buddies in the rest of the world, summer doesn't end until October. They, on the other hand, are looking ahead to sweaters in September and jeans right after Labor Day.

Not true for those of us who have chosen this latitude.

Our sunglasses fog immediately and completely as soon as we exit an air-conditioned building.

Heat escapes from the car in a dreadful and visible wave, and we spend hours looking for parking places in the shade.

Air conditioners drip and hum from windows all over the island spawning mental debates that pit comfort against cost.

Do we leave the air on while we're out of the house, or shut it off until we return?

Sure, we'll save a few bucks on next month's bill, (I actually remembered to write Keys Energy Services, and not City Electric on my check this month) but there's not much that can compare to the feeling of pure, unadulterated relief that hits the skin in that first blast of cool that accompanies the opening of a door to an air-conditioned apartment.

It's wasteful and slightly more expensive, but it's immediate and it's wonderful.

The smell of downtown garbage cans in the heat, on the other hand, is just as immediate, but not so wonderful.

Divers eagerly plunge into the depths seeking not only marine life, but the sensation of cooler water that greets them as soon as there's more than 20 feet of saltwater between them and the scorching surface.

Frozen drinks on Duval Street don't stay that way for long, and condensation beads up instantly on the side of a glass, from which it starts to drip on coffee tables, laps and chins.

Some of us, at this time of year, opt for pants over shorts to avoid the searing pain that comes from trying to get out of a chair too quickly once the skin on the back of our thighs has become permanently affixed to the seat.

By now, there's no pool anywhere with water that's actually refreshing, and we brush our teeth in the morning with water the temperature of bath water because that's what comes out of the faucet.

Your clothes become crumpled and soggy the minute you step outside, and every part of exposed flesh starts to burn.

It is in these weeks every year that our friends in cooler climates actually enjoy asking us about the weather down here. They usually do it begrudgingly in the winter and end up aggravated by our smug answer about the February sunshine.

But in August and September they love talking about low humidity and cool breezes – both just a distant memory and hope for the future down here.

Never fear, our smug friends will be stomping their feet against the wintry blasts in no time at all.

"Man, it's cold out here."

"Come on inside, where it's warm."

We won't have to have those conversations. We won't have to find missing gloves, wear two pairs of socks and grip a freezing steering wheel in an arctic car whose heater only blows cold air until the engine is warm.

We have only to wait a few more weeks for that first cool breeze of October – a sigh of relief that whispers across town and seems to reach everyone simultaneously. We look up, look around and breathe deeply. We'll survive, we always do.

August 18, 2002

SPECIAL THANKS

There are certain people whose help and involvement made this book a reality and one worth reading.

Thanks a million to Kerry Karshna, graphic designer extraordinaire, who was able to turn a bunch of smeared newspaper columns into a great looking book.

Thanks and a big sigh of relief for Emily Roach and Andrea Anapol, friends and expert proofreaders who saved me from several years – and thousands of copies – of embarrassment.

Thanks also to Terry Schmida, friend and editor, who graciously gives me space on the left side of a newspaper page every other Sunday.

And to my publisher John Cooke, Jr., who first gave me the opportunity to write a column and then gave me permission to publish a book of them. Thanks, John.

ABOUT THE AUTHOR

Aside from a short and landlocked stint in a few of those Midwestern rectangle states when she was too young to know any better, Mandy Bolen grew up in Ocean City at the South Jersey shore.

When not serving food and drinks to tourists who requested Jimmy Buffett tunes, she spent every summer perfecting her skills at lying perfectly still on a canvas beach chair positioned directly under the sun.

Sometime during a college spring break trip to Key West that no one remembers all that clearly, Mandy realized there was a place where it was summer all year long.

In Key West, there were even more tourists requesting Jimmy Buffett tunes, but she was no longer bringing them cheeseburgers and margaritas.

Mandy got a job as a reporter and columnist for the Key West Citizen daily newspaper and began writing about the town and climate that had beckoned. Cold drinks and colorful people in a hot town have provided enough education, insight and insanity to keep her notebook filled. People seemed to like what she wrote, so she kept doing it.

But she hasn't lost her talent for lying perfectly still on a reclined canvas beach chair – and she has the tan lines to prove it.

Also available from Phantom Press
www.phantompress.com

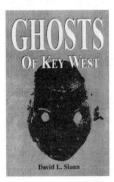 

*A collection of the newspaper
columns that keep Key West laughing.*